Dedication

Life is a head game in the mind—but the mind of Christ overcomes and restores our mindset to the sound mind that is ours in Christ. This study guide is dedicated to you, dear readers, that your mind will be renewed as you read and apply the beautiful truths contained in the accompanying book and in this study guide. In the back of this study guide are additional resources to help you overcome the battle of negative mindsets. We are cheering you on in the battle!

Table of Contents

Introduction

"Set your minds on things that are above, not on things that are on earth."

Colossians 3:2, ESV

Our minds can be set on thoughts that lead us far away from Christ and we might not even be aware of it. Mindsets are a part of our belief system that is shaped by our experiences and the surrounding culture. We can have strong opinions that are already formed based on the background we came from. Or we can experience mindset changes from our emotions. Either way we are not a victim of our mindsets, and the renewal of our minds is not merely changing our minds by positive thinking but transforming our minds through righteous thinking. We can experience a mindset reset as we learn to align our thoughts with God's, not ours. The mind is the seat of our emotions and will ultimately lead us away from Christ unless we choose to set our mind on God's way, not ours. If we are to win the battle of the mind, we need to recognize that we can make up our mind as we saturate our minds in God's Word. We have the mind of Christ.

This study guide used in conjunction with the book *Make Up Your Mind* will take you through ten negative mindsets and help you apply the principles in the book as we do a deeper biblical dive into each of the mindsets. This study guide incorporates the corresponding chapter in *Make Up Your Mind*, five days of application, and one day of rest in each week.

Begin each week reading through the assigned chapter for the unit/week. Use the application section in the book and jot down how God speaks to your heart as you work through the study. There is space to do this in the study guide. Use the suggested schedule on the next page to guide your study time. We have intentionally sought to include a few questions in the study guide each day to keep you engaged with the chapter, without overwhelming you with work. In this way, we pray that you are able to apply what you are reading in the book and participate consistently.

Retraining your brain, just like any other muscle, will take time. The Counselor's Corner provides an opportunity at the end of each week to do this.

A special note to small group leaders: download our free Leader's Guide to help you as you lead your weekly small group. You can download the Leader's Guide here: https://www.randallhouse.com/product-downloads/.

Weekly Schedule

Preparation: Each week begins by reading the corresponding chapter from *Make Up Your Mind*, followed by five days of daily Bible study.

Complete Study Guide Day 1

Complete Study Guide Day 2

Complete Study Guide Day 3

Complete Study Guide Day 4

Complete Study Guide Day 5 and Counselor's Corner

Rest

WEEK ONE

"When Elijah heard it, he covered his face with his robe and went out and stood at the entrance to the cave. All of a sudden a voice asked him, 'Why are you here, Elijah?'"

1 Kings 19:13 NET

Chapter 1

Why Are You Here?

"Answer me, O Lord, answer me, that this people may know that you, O Lord, are God, and that you have turned their hearts back."
1 Kings 18:37 ESV

My husband tells me I need a GPS to get out of our driveway. A bit snarky of a comment if you ask me, and DEFINITELY exaggerated, but the truth is, I've got issues when it comes to directions. Even after I have driven somewhere I might not be able to tell you how I got there. So don't ask this girl for directions when it comes to driving. While navigating a vehicle is important, the most important navigation happens in our mind. If we are not manning the gate in our mind, we can travel far away to a place we did not intend.

Perhaps you have not given a lot of thought to negative mindsets. It is easy to make excuses for them. Perhaps you've heard of a few: "He made me angry," "I couldn't help myself," or "It is just my personality." Don't believe any of those lies. No one makes us do anything. And we are not stuck with a certain bent in our way of thinking. Other people can cause us to stumble and make it hard for us to overcome negative mindsets, for sure, but no one makes us think the thoughts we think. That is our choice. Whether or not we feel empowered to make that choice, it is part of what God gave to us with free will and the Holy Spirit to help us walk in the Spirit rather than the flesh.

Reading the story about Elijah was startling to me. This was an incredible man of God. In 1 Kings 18 he asked God to prove that He could change the mind of man. Then in 1 Kings 19, he allowed his own mind to succumb to and be defeated by fear. The story in 1 Kings 19 was supposed to end differently. Elijah was supposed to have an "aha moment" and overcome. God did ask him twice, after all, about how he had gotten to where he was. God knew the cause of Elijah's struggle. Elijah thought he knew, but discouragement and fear clouded his vision and seemed insurmountable.

The battle of the mind is never done. Sorry to disappoint you if you hoped that once you learned how to fight the negative mindsets that it would mean no more mindset battles. But when we know how to fight the battles of the mind with the Word of God and how to operate in the mind of Christ, we can overcome. This companion study guide is an opportunity for you to apply the principles from the book, *Make Up Your Mind*. You can make up your mind, friend—one thought at a time.

In each chapter of this book there is space for you to write notes from your chapter reading and then space for you to answer the reflection questions in this book and any subsequent thoughts God is placing on your heart.

Day One: Are You Wandering?

*"But I am afraid that, as the serpent deceived
Eve by his trickery, your minds will be led astray
from sincere and pure devotion to Christ."*
2 Corinthians 11:3 NASB

We are all prone to wander, but we are often not aware that we are in fact, wandering. Our own hearts are deceitful (Jeremiah 17:9) and the negative mindsets we are afflicted by distract us with worries and point us away from God's grace. From the least of us to the greatest, everyone will have to do battle with their own thoughts if they are to live the abundant life Christ promises.

If anyone had a mindset of faith and boldness, it was Elijah. Yet even his mindset was distracted and pulled away from pure devotion to God's plan. Elijah prophesied that there would be no rain for three years and it was so. He raised a young boy from the dead. He challenged 450 prophets of Baal and 400 prophets of Asherah to a spiritual duel of sorts, inviting them to worship the one, true God. The living God answered by fire. Talk about a bold witness for God. Elijah's resumé was a standout as far as the impact he was having. What caused his mindset to shift so that he wandered from the passionate faith he had? We can do amazing things like Elijah when our mindset is filled with faith, fixed on God's purposes.

18

READ 1 KINGS 18:36–39.

What had Elijah asked God to do in verse 37?

_____

_____

How many people's minds were changed to believe in God when fire came down from Heaven?

_____

_____

Elijah asked God to demonstrate His presence so the people would have their hearts changed and know God. God answered in a big way. All the people responded. And then He prayed, and it rained. It would seem there was nothing that Elijah could not do. But mindsets can shift. Despite the great miracles God did through Elijah, it would be a woman who would send Elijah running in fear.

READ 1 KINGS 19:1–4.

What did Jezebel threaten to do to Elijah?

_____

_____

Where did Elijah go?

_____

_____

The wilderness is a place of confusion. It is where we wander seemingly with no direction. It is a place of testing. Moses and the people of Israel wandered in the wilderness after the parting of the Red Sea. They would stay there awhile—40 years instead of 11 days. Getting out of the wilderness is tricky if we aren't clear minded. Jesus went to the wilderness willingly to be tested. His mind was set on God and His Word. And He left the wilderness quickly. His preparation for the wilderness was fasting and praying. The wilderness requires us to operate in the Spirit rather than the flesh.

Elijah, who had been so clear about his mission before, let his mindset drift and lead him to a place of desperation. I don't think any of us choose the wilderness when we are in our right mind. But the wilderness is where we wander when we go off the path of righteousness and are led by our heart rather than the mind of Christ. Disillusionment and fear, the chief culprits behind many of the mindsets, keep us bound in the wilderness, but faith helps us find our way again.

Do you have a wilderness experience in your own life right now? Have you wandered off the path God has for you? Pray and ask God if you have wandered away from His purposes. Write it down below.

_____

_____

Of the ten mindsets, which mindset do you think contributed to your wandering?

_____

_____

Tomorrow we will look at a common root behind all the negative mindsets and unmask the real enemy. We don't have to wander in our thoughts when our God is for us and with us.

Day Two: The Root of Elijah's Mindset Shift

> *"Fear not, for I am with you; be not dismayed,*
> *for I am your God; I will strengthen you,*
> *I will help you, I will uphold you*
> *with my righteous right hand."*
> Isaiah 41:10 ESV

Common to all the negative mindsets is fear. Fear is a powerful tool of the devil that can cause a shift in our thinking. We don't want something to happen. So rather than stopping and assessing our thoughts, we shrink back. We forget that God is greater than any fear or problem we are facing. He doesn't change. We do. By caving to our thoughts and fears instead of taking those thoughts captive and submitting them to the truth of God's Word and the mind of Christ, we become prey to negative mindsets. Elijah's fear of Jezebel's threats finally unnerved Elijah and broke through his mindset that had been previously fixed on faith in God.

READ 1 KINGS 18:13–15.

When Obadiah told Elijah about the persecution Jezebel was inflicting on God's prophets, what was Elijah's response?

_____

_____

If Elijah did not allow Jezebel's persecution of the prophets of God to throw him into a mindset of fear in 1 Kings 18, what caused him to give in to fear with Jezebel's threat in 1 Kings 19:2?

_____

_____

How did Elijah's focus change from the first instance of Jezebel's threats to the second?

_____

_____

Jezebel's original threat was concerning all of God's prophets, of which Elijah was one. But Jezebel's second threat was personal. It was directed solely at Elijah. Have you ever been targeted by someone? It might be as simple as someone disliking you and gossiping about you. You might be excluded or worse, directly insulted. And then things get ramped up real fast when threats come. Oh, how I remember this on the school yard in a town I lived in where I was constantly threatened to be beaten up. Fights were the norm in that place, but when it got personal, fear was born. I can understand Elijah's fear, but how I wish he would have stood firm as before. The shift in mindset did not permit him to apply the same faith to his fear that he applied when he boldly challenged close to 1,000 people as the only prophet.

What are you afraid of?

_____

_____

Fear can drive us to run away from God. But if we think rationally and truthfully through our fears, we realize that we gain the victory by facing our fears with faith—not running from them. Consider where you are in your mind right now. What is your mindset toward your present circumstances? Like Elijah, do you wonder how you got to where you are? Tomorrow we will look at our belief system and the impact that doubt can have on our faith and mindset.

Day Three: What Are You Believing?

> "In spite of all this, they kept on sinning; in spite of his wonders, they did not believe."
> Psalm 78:32 NIV

Along with fear, another powerful weapon common to all mindsets is unbelief. If the enemy of our souls can get us to doubt God, our mind becomes his playground. The story of the Israelites' unbelief throughout the pages of Scripture is painful to read when we consider all God did for them. How could they drift from the One Who loved them and rescued them? Mindset. One would think we could control our own thoughts, but friends, it is a battle. And we must engage in this battle of the mind in order to overcome.

When we don't believe that God can help us with our negative mindsets, this is ultimately unbelief that we need to repent of. Our belief system is under attack with the various negative mindsets. We are ultimately living what we are believing. Paramount to overcoming negative mindsets is protecting our belief system.

Elijah's boldness revealed his bold faith, but a mindset shift exposed a breach in his belief system. His faith in God was breached by his fear of Jezebel. Sometimes our problems become so large in our own eyes that we struggle to have faith to overcome. Like the question that God repeated to Elijah, if we have a plan of accountability with questions to remind us of what we believe, we can hold onto our beliefs and not stray.

READ 1 KINGS 19:2–8.

In 1 Kings 19, God still had the same power Elijah spoke of in 1 Kings 18, but Elijah doubted. God even met Elijah by miraculously taking care of him. Proof enough? Yes. But when our mind is made up to give in to negative mindsets, we cannot make up our mind to have faith. What doubts do you have about God? What promises in Scripture refute those doubts? Record them below.

_____

_____

How has God provided for you even as you struggled in your own negative mindsets?

_____

_____

Not admitting our doubts just keeps them housed in our brains. Like Elijah, we can repeat the narrative in our mind and try to find our own solutions, relying on ourselves only to become trapped in our own thoughts. But letting God's Word trump our own solutions and mindset fixes is the only way to healing our mindsets. Don't let your feelings dictate your faith. What solutions are you ready to lay down?

_____

_____

Day Four: Excuses, Excuses

"We destroy arguments and every lofty opinion raised against the knowledge of God and take every thought captive to obey Christ."
2 Corinthians 10:5 ESV

Sometimes in this life we feel like we just can't catch a break. We become good at excuses rather than operating in faith. Maybe you are familiar with some of the common excuses. I got angry because . . . I was afraid because . . .

"But" or "because" are those little words that make us feel better about ourselves while we sidestep to a negative mindset. We might be covered by our excuses, but excuses don't heal our minds or hearts. We need to capture thoughts that threaten to wreck our lives and subject them to the will of God and mind of Christ.

Elijah's excuses are like our own, looking to our weaknesses or circumstances as a disability rather than relying on God's strength. Elijah's situation was dire, for sure, but God had proven Himself to Elijah and everyone in the land in mighty ways through Elijah.

READ 1 KINGS 19:9–10.

Why do you think God asked Elijah a question He already knew the answer to?

_____

_____

What was the focus of Elijah's answer?

_____

_____

Elijah's focus on himself overrode what God had done in Elijah's mind. Shifting from God's ability to our own ability is a surefire way of leading us to fear. Is there anything in your life that you are tempted to view through your inability or ability over God's?

_____

_____

Elijah offered excuses. Excuses are not a real solution. They are, in fact, a lie. And a cheap substitute for God's best. What excuses are you making for negative mindsets in your life?

_____

_____

This is real heart work we are accomplishing in here, friends. Hang in there! Our mindsets will be free to dwell in the Spirit rather than the flesh when we learn how to have the mind of Christ. That's the topic for tomorrow. Don't forget to read chapter one in *Make Up Your Mind* and take the mindset quiz!

Day Five: Putting on the Mind of Christ

> *"'For who has understood the mind*
> *of the Lord so as to instruct him?'*
> *But we have the mind of Christ."*
> 1 Corinthians 2:16 ESV

In each chapter of *Make Up Your Mind*, we will be looking at the mind of Christ and how Christ responded to the temptation of negative mindsets. Scripture says we have the mind of Christ, but it seems that often we are not faithfully walking in that mindset. Part of the problem is we have "Christianese" or semantics that we don't really understand. The mind of Christ is one such example. The mind of Christ is the goal but not the means. It is Christ's thoughts borne out in our lives as we immerse and saturate our mind in His Word. Ultimately, the more we are in God's Word, the more we will be able to recognize counterfeit thoughts and to think like Christ. Recognizing wrong thoughts helps us to put off wrong thinking and to embrace right thinking.

READ PSALM 116:1–4.

Compare the Psalmist's response to death threats with Elijah's response in **1 Kings 19:4.**

What did the Psalmist and Elijah have in common?

How did they differ in their response?

Both cried out to God, but both did not believe.

NOW READ 1 KINGS 19:11–14.

God met Elijah with His presence yet Elijah dug in his heels and committed to his original narrative. What was God trying to communicate to Elijah by showing His presence?

God is real. He is more real than the thoughts pumping through our mind. When we know Him and understand how awesome He is, we don't waste time on futile thoughts that are so far beneath Him. The mind of Christ is an invitation to us all to think on a higher level. Don't let fear or unbelief eclipse God's power. Nothing we go through in this life is beyond His aid. We have the presence of God when we accept Jesus' salvation. God is in us, for us, and with us. God is always near, friend. How does God's presence change your view of the problems in your mind?

_____

_____

We live our best life when we have the Mind of Christ over matter. Let's make up our mind to believe God is who He says He is and that He is able to help us. He Who promised is faithful. Let's not question God but question our thoughts and drill down to the real strongholds instead.

After you have read chapter one in the book, answer the reflection questions on the next page in your small group and share any insights you have from this week in your group time.

Make Up Your Mind (Study Guide)

Weekly Wrap-Up

Chapter One Reflection Questions

Which trigger did you identify with the most?

_____

_____

Which tip is your "go to strategy" when it comes to overcoming negative mindsets?

_____

_____

What does it mean to you to have the mind of Christ?

_____

_____

The Keys to Mindset Hacks

Write down the keys from chapter one and any other insight that was significant to you!

Key Thought

_____

_____

Key Verse

_____

_____

Key Change

_____

_____

Quiz Results

_____

_____

Counselor's Corner

Mindset Reset

Mindset Meditation

"Do not conform to the pattern of this world, but be transformed by the renewing of your mind. Then you will be able to test and approve what God's will is— his good, pleasing and perfect will."
Romans 12:2 NIV

One way to meditate is to focus deeply on a specific passage of Scripture or phrase. You might want to set a timer before you begin. Choose a comfortable position as you spend this time connecting with God through His Word. I like to choose a stretching position wearing loose clothing in the morning or at night. I often play instrumental worship music while doing this exercise.

Take a couple of deep breaths in through your nose and out through your mouth. Spend a few moments tensing a muscle in your body and then releasing that muscle. Meditate on Romans 12:2, allowing God to bring to mind images, word associations or biblical truths. I've shared some examples below.

Transformed – change, healing, hope, Heaven

Renewing – better, changing, fresh daily

Mind – my brain, thoughts, wisdom, what I think, focus

God's will – not a bullseye, practices like giving thanks, praying without ceasing, encouraging others

Good – makes me happy, smile on my face, blessed, lighthearted, God

Pleasing – happy, satisfied, content, fully relaxed

Perfect – only God, I don't have to be, not this world, Heaven

On the lines below, describe your meditation experience.

_____

_____

_____

Mindset Movement

What verse did you choose? _____

Describe some of the places you chose to say the verse aloud resetting your mindset.

_____

_____

_____

_____

Questions for Connection

1. Share the verse or phrase you chose for the mindset movement.
2. What battles do you feel like you may be losing in your mind?
3. How does knowing that God is bigger than your problem or situation give you hope?
4. What could change in your life if you retrained your brain daily for a year?

Additional Resources

Switch On Your Brain: The Key to Peak Happiness, Thinking, and Health by Dr. Caroline Leaf

Get Out of Your Head: Stopping the Spiral of Toxic Thoughts by Jennie Allen

Notes or Questions from Chapter Reading

_____

_____

_____

_____

_____

_____

_____

_____

_____

_____

_____

_____

_____

_____

WEEK TWO

"Because you did not believe in me, to uphold me as holy in the eyes of the people of Israel, therefore you shall not bring this assembly into the land that I have given them."

Numbers 20:10b-12 ESV

Chapter 2

 *The Angry Mindset—Battling Bitterness and Unforgiveness*

*"Human anger does not produce
the righteousness God desires."*
James 1:20 NLT

Temper tantrums aren't just for toddlers, evidently. Adults are just as capable of losing their cool. Even if we don't have an anger problem, we still need to know how to manage anger. The presence of anger in our lives is the presence of a bitter root or an offense. It needs to be dealt with, so we are not bound in unforgiveness.

Frankly, I get it that Moses was worn out and sick and tired of hearing the whining all around him. Parents know all about dealing with complaining. But what amazes me about Moses is the fact that we don't hear his voice complaining about God's provision like the Israelites were. Hanging around complainers can tend to impact us and make us want to complain, too.

In Numbers 11, we see the complaint of Moses, which was quite different from the complaint of the Israelites. The Israelites complained "in the hearing of the LORD." They did not complain to God. But Moses did. Moses was real with God. It is what we do with our disappointments, anger, and hurt that makes all the difference. If we come to God, He can give us the grace we need to turn from anger.

Moses' sin wasn't necessarily the anger itself but forgetting the holiness of God. When God disciplined him, we do not hear him complain when he was called out for his sin. Perhaps we, too, forget the holiness of God when we give full vent to our anger. Anger keeps us from doing God's work. And we who have been forgiven our offenses have no right to hold an offense against anyone else.

Day One: What Provokes You?

"Good sense makes one slow to anger, and it is his glory to overlook an offense."
Proverbs 19:11 ESV

Next to fear and doubt, being offended is also a catalyst behind many negative mindsets. Offenses happen when we fixate on something that is negative. An example of this is when we are offended by presuming others' thoughts about us, causing us to nurse grudges. Or when we meditate on something that someone did that hurt our feelings. The Israelites complained some 14+ times as recorded in Scripture. These were moments when they vented complaints—raising a big stink and accusation against God and Moses.

READ EXODUS 5:19–21.

What made the Israelite overseers angry?

_____

_____

Any of us would be angry at unjust treatment, but there was something deeper here. The Israelites were angry at the way in which God was delivering them. And God's representatives weren't doing such a hot job in their estimation. This hits close to home, doesn't it? Complaints rise within church walls when congregants complain about how things are getting done. Church politics are at the base of dysfunction in the body of Christ, and it emanates from being offended that we did not get our way. The color of the carpet. The choice of music. Irritation and unforgiveness of another believer we hold hostage in our mind with unforgiveness. But sometimes we can legitimately be suffering, and it can be tempting to also complain and become angry when life is simply just hard. What then?

READ EXODUS 14:10–14.

See the doubt and fear working in their mindsets? What was Moses' answer to their complaints?

_____

_____

Complaining is an accusation against God that His plans and provision are not enough. Complaining comes from an entitlement mentality. It says we deserve better than what we were given. It is an attitude of offense and frankly, is offensive. We can be provoked when we let ourselves be offended at God for allowing the suffering in. But at the root of offense is a misunderstanding. We did not get what we deserve. We deserved hell and damnation and God gave grace and forgiveness instead. We will all endure hardship in this life and be mistreated by others in a fallen world. But the One Who covered our offenses enables us to let go of the offenses that bind and blind our mindsets.

On and on Moses endured the "hangry" Israelites who were hungry, thirsty, and sinning left and right, and then it happened. Moses had had enough and he was provoked to an angry mindset. Anger begets anger, doesn't it?

What is it that provokes you to anger?

_____

_____

Tomorrow we will dive into what led to the provocation of anger and start to find solutions. Thank God that His anger toward us was quelled by His undeserved grace and mercy!

"For his anger lasts only a moment, but his favor lasts a lifetime. . ." (Psalm 30:5, NLT).

Day Two: Go Down Moses

*"Trust in the Lord with all your heart, and do not
lean on your own understanding."*
Proverbs 3:5 ESV

Moses was miraculously saved by God as an infant and miraculously chosen by God to save God's people. We can almost hear the victorious background music, can't we? But Moses had to go back to a place that he had previously escaped from. Doubt and fear were trying to dissuade Moses from following his calling. Known as the humblest man on earth (Numbers 12:3), anger did not define Moses. This is what makes Moses' display of anger surprising. Any of us can unleash the green monster of ire if we do not keep our mindset in check. When our mindset is fixed on God and not ourselves, we are able to navigate negative mindsets and problems that arise.

READ EXODUS 3:7–12.

What was Moses' mindset and focus driven by?

_____

_____

What was God's response?

_____

_____

When God called Moses, Moses focused on his inability. God tried to get Moses' mindset to shift to God's ability. God is the great I AM. Nothing is too difficult for Him. We won't find the answers to our broken negative mindsets in ourselves. We will only restore our mindsets as we focus on God. Moses could not do the calling of God with his own abilities or strength. Neither can we. Anger will mount as we frustratingly try to accomplish what only God can. Doubts can creep back in when we focus on our ability.

READ EXODUS 3:13–14.

The "what if's" can paralyze us from moving forward in this life, keeping us stuck in mindsets. What was Moses' real question?

_____

_____

Moses needed something more than a word from God. He wanted to know that the mission he was going on would not fail. Moses was sent on a mission impossible, apart from God. But God met him there. With every weakness he admitted, he was given God's strength and ability. Sometimes anger arises in our lives because of the difficulties we encounter. We didn't expect the problems that come our way. Tomorrow we will take a look at how to turn our whining into winning. Or perhaps other people's whining into a win.

Day Three: Stop Your Whining!

*"Do everything without complaining and
arguing, so that no one can criticize you . . ."*
Philippians 2:14-15a NLT

Anger is aroused when complaining is rampant. It's just plain annoying and wears down those listening to it. Inherent within the whiner is an entitled attitude that lacks gratitude. Complaining is not just unpleasant to listen to, it is rebellion. It is hard not to take complaining personally. It feels like an affront against us. But someone else's anger is not about us, and it is really an indicator of the bondage that person is in. Our response to their anger can help to quell their anger or perhaps even ignite our own.

READ NUMBERS 20:2–5.

How did the people gather against Moses and Aaron? What was their chief complaint?

_____

_____

READ NUMBERS 10:10.

How did God handle their grumbling?

_____

_____

When the Israelites were whining, they were in opposition and rebellion to God. The manner of their complaining was sinful, too. The Israelites did not ultimately trust God or God's leaders. If we are honest, we have been whiners from time to time like the Israelites, too. When we give in to whining rather than choosing to trust God, we don't win. We win when we release our anger by letting go of control. Satisfaction for an angry person is elusive. But we can learn how to manage our expectations and release the control we think we have and that's the subject we are discussing tomorrow.

Day Four: Releasing Control

> *"Let all bitterness and wrath and anger*
> *and clamor and slander be put away*
> *from you, along with all malice."*
> Ephesians 4:31 ESV

While we can try to control outcomes and people and events in our lives, sometimes controlling our own thoughts and mindsets is the hardest thing. Paul uses the operative word "let" when it comes to letting go of the anger that controls us. We do not have to be controlled by resentful, angry, or bitter feelings or thoughts. We release control when we accept God's control over our lives.

Managing our expectations can also help us to open our tight-fisted wants from life and from others. The Israelites wanted God's deliverance, but they wanted it their way. In one of THE most painful seasons of MY life, when everything in my life was falling apart, I desperately wanted to make sense of it all and to regain control. But in reality, I never had control in the first place.

READ NUMBERS 20:6–12.

What had God asked Moses to do?

_____

_____

Why did Moses respond in the way he did?

_____

_____

Moses' weariness from the quarreling of the Israelites led to an angry response as he attempted to regain control of an unruly people. How do you handle the unruly people in your life?

_____

_____

READ NUMBERS 20:13.

Who were the unruly Israelites really contending with?

_____

_____

Sometimes our anger can be quelled when we realize that other people's anger with us is really against God. We might just be the messenger, but either way, our response to their anger might help them turn their bitterness into forgiveness and trust in God or stir their wrath up more. Tomorrow we will look at how to humbly deal with the rabble rousers in our midst and perhaps even look in the mirror and let go of the anger that has a hold on us.

Day Five: A Culture of Humility

"A gentle answer turns away wrath, but a harsh word stirs up anger."
Proverbs 15:1 NIV

Sometimes it is the people who we do life with who can irk us the most. We rub elbows with them when we don't feel well, when we are sad, and in all the struggles of life. They see the grumpiest side of us just as we do of them. But those who know us best should see our best side, not our worst. God wisely chose a shepherd to lead His people. Moses truly had a patient, shepherd's heart. And so should we when we care for the souls of people we profess to love.

READ EXODUS 32:30-32.

What did Moses ask God to do when he discovered the Israelites had sinned?

_____

_____

God was angry with the Israelites. Perhaps after all Moses had put up with, it would have been reasonable for Moses to tell the LORD to zap them. But Moses asked God to blot his own name out of the book so that the people might be saved. He pleads on their behalf. He loved them more than being offended by them. Do we love others more than our pride? Love can help extinguish anger. Just as God so loved the world that He came and bore His anger on our behalf by placing it on His beloved Son. Forgiveness sets us free from the bondage anger brings. We are no better than those we are angry with.

READ EXODUS 32:21.

Moses came down from the mountain to find God's people in the middle of revelry and idolatry. Who did Moses blame for the people's sins?

_____

_____

Moses cast blame on Aaron who should have led the people away from sin rather than giving in to their sin. Humility and understanding reveal the real cause of anger and sin. Moses knew God's people were prone to wander, argue, and complain in anger, and he fiercely protected them and led them anyway. Love your tribe fiercely, friends. When they offend and get angry, love them anyway and lead them to forgiveness. We get to establish the culture we live in. Establish a culture of grace that helps soften mindsets and lead them to the cross where we are all desperate for God to give us the victory over our own thoughts.

Weekly Wrap-Up

Chapter Two Reflection Questions

Which trigger do you identify with the most?

_____

_____

Which tip do you think you will use most to overcome the angry mindset?

_____

_____

How did Christ handle anger?

_____

_____

The Keys to Mindset Hacks

Write down the keys from chapter two and any other insight that was significant to you.

Key Thought

_____

_____

Key Verse

_____

_____

Key Change

_____

_____

Counselor's Corner

Battling Anger

Mindset Meditation

"My dear brothers and sisters, take note of this: Everyone should be quick to listen, slow to speak and slow to become angry, because human anger does not produce the righteousness that God desires."
James 1:19-20 NIV

In our minds, we can practice the changes we want to make in our lives by using imagery. Take several deep breaths—filling your lungs so you can see your chest rise up and down, up and down, up and down. Make sure you are in a comfortable position as you envision yourself in the three situations below:

1. See yourself listening with your full attention while someone talks.
2. See yourself taking a moment of pause before speaking or responding to someone who matters to you.

3. See yourself tempted to become angry and then pausing and using your calm down skills to harness that anger or even let it go before responding.

Record on the lines below what you visualized and how it felt to practice these biblical skills.

_____

_____

_____

Mindset Movement

Describe on the lines below a scenario where you showed yourself or someone else compassion.

_____

_____

_____

Questions for Connection

1. Share with the group whether you struggle more with showing yourself or others compassion.
2. Describe your anger style and how it has been helpful or harmful to you.
3. What is a "should" you tell yourself that you will work on turning into a "could" this week?
4. Share a situation in your life that you could create freedom for yourself by practicing self-compassion and accepting the grace God has already given you centuries ago on the cross.

Additional Resources

Self Compassion: The Proven Power of Being Kind to Yourself by Dr. Kristen Neff

https://self-compassion.org (take the quiz and see how well you tend to demonstrate self-compassion toward yourself)

Change Your Brain, Change Your Life (Revised and Expanded): The Breakthrough Program for Conquering Anxiety, Depression, Obsessiveness, Lack of Focus, Anger, and Memory Problems by Daniel G. Amen

Notes or Questions from Chapter Reading

_____

_____

_____

_____

_____

_____

_____

_____

_____

_____

_____

_____

_____

_____

_____

_____

_____

_____

WEEK THREE

"Cast all your anxiety on him, because he cares for you."

1 Peter 5:7 NIV

Chapter 3

The Anxious Mindset— Battling Fear and Worry, Restoring Peace

"When my anxious thoughts multiply within me,
Your comfort delights my soul."
Psalm 94:19 NASB

God does not want us to be anxious. Christ came to give us peace (John 14:27). But sometimes that peace can be hard to come by. Anxiety is not just for the anxious and it comes in many forms. Worry happens over the many uncertain outcomes and challenges life brings. Fear arises from unexpected circumstances. But even in the multitude of anxieties that can abound in a fallen world, there is a place of refuge for those who choose it.

Anxiety says God is not in control of our life or world, so we need to take control. Anxiety says we are not seen by God or that no one cares. Anxiety is focused on the problems of life rather than on the Lord over our lives. It is easy to see why anxiety comes so naturally. It is a fleshly response to a multitude of triggers easily found in a fallen world. It is natural to respond to stimuli that proclaims there is a problem with no solution. For this is the backbone of anxiety—there is little to no hope, and *we* must figure out a solution.

Jehoshaphat's response to three nations attacking him is a beautiful example of what faith can do to our anxiety. It would be odd not to respond to such a threat, but how he responded reveals the power available to those who don't try to handle anxious moments in their own strength. It is not lost on me that the enemies were descendants of Lot. Sometimes attacks come from familiar places that perhaps we did not expect. But nothing surprises God. We will have to battle unbelief and doubt to break free of anxiety and Jehoshaphat teaches us how to do that.

But this week we will not just look at anxiety that occurs from situations. There are different types of anxieties that we need to recognize and deal with biblically. Social anxiety, the fear of failure and insecurity, to name a few. Anxiety does not have to be the boss of us.

Day One: What is the Root of Your Anxiety?

*"Peace I leave with you; my peace I give
to you. Not as the world gives do I give to you.
Let not your hearts be troubled,
neither let them be afraid."
John 14:27 ESV*

Anxiety is the symptom, but underneath the surface is the true cause of our anxiety. The roots of anxiety are many, including circumstances, traumatic events, mindset patterns, and health diagnoses. Our emotional response to anxiety-producing events and circumstances will determine whether we give in to anxiety or rise above it. Our emotions do not have to have the final say. We can inform our mind rather than having our mind inform us. When we know how to handle feelings of anxiety biblically, we can get to the root of the problem and choose peace.

READ 2 CHRONICLES 20:1–2.

What surprise attack are you encountering in your life right now or have you encountered?

_____

_____

What steps are you taking, or did you take to handle the anxiety you felt?

_____

_____

Sometimes the root of our anxiety is situational, as in the battle that Jehoshaphat was facing. But how we process that anxiety can either suppress it or cause it to grow. Anxiety can make us want to run to others for comfort and influence. Sometimes we can become more anxious by talking about what is making us anxious.

Jehoshaphat used his influence to lead others to the throne room of God. He did not run to the people for answers but led them to God. Sometimes the root of our anxiety is because we think the battle is ours, or we don't talk with God about it. Anxiety is silenced when we put faith in God's ability rather than focusing on the problem. Tomorrow we will dive in to find out how to handle anxiety in its many varied forms.

Day Two: Jehoshaphat's Perspective

"For God gave us a spirit not of fear but of power and love and self-control."
2 Timothy 1:7 ESV

Whenever we encounter fear, we can be sure it is not from God. But our perspective on the fear we are having can be changed in the presence of God and help us to defeat anxiety rather than being overcome by it. When our perspective is shaped by faith rather than fear, we are no longer just playing with a defensive strategy in the battle of our mind, but an offensive one.

READ 2 CHRONICLES 20:3–4.

How did Jehoshaphat handle his initial moments of anxiety with the people who surrounded him?

_____

_____

What does Jehoshaphat's response teach us about our emotions?

_____

_____

Emotions create within us a powerful adrenaline response that typically triggers fight or flight. Sometimes we can feel as if we do not have any power to affect our emotions, but this is a lie from the enemy. Jehoshaphat felt the anxiety strongly—to the point of sheer terror. And he knew where his help came from. Jehoshaphat controlled his emotions rather than allowing his emotions to control him.

What is your perspective on the emotions you feel during anxiety? Do you feel they are legitimate?

_____

_____

What coping mechanisms do you use when you feel anxious?

_____

_____

Are you willing to give that anxiety to God to take care of? He is better at handling it. That work situation that bugs you, or family situation that fills you with a sense of being out of control—maybe that is the best place, after all, for us to be out of control. When we try to control things, we sure can make a mess. Letting our feelings and perspective be altered in the presence of God and letting go of control frees us to not be controlled by anxiety. It can be hard to let go of anxiety. We might not feel that we can but naming our fear and crying out to God empowers us to realize that we do get to choose. We might not be able to fix our situations or anxious feelings, but through Christ, we can have peace in the midst as we trust God is in control.

Day Three: Facing Your Fears

"Have I not commanded you? Be strong and courageous. Do not be frightened, and do not be dismayed, for the Lord your God is with you wherever you go."
Joshua 1:9 ESV

Facing fear rather than running from it helps us overcome anxiety. Fear must be faced and defeated, or it will cripple and limit us. Sometimes anxiety gets the upper hand because we don't face it—we let it control us, instead. Recognizing the battle we are truly in, helps us know how to fight.

READ 2 CHRONICLES 20:15.

Whose battle was it anyway?

_____

_____

Anxiety is a battle of the mind that tries to corner us into using our own resources as we struggle for relief. But knowing that our God is indeed for us and that He wants to fight our battles for us helps us face our fears differently.

Make Up Your Mind (Study Guide)

READ 2 CHRONICLES 17:3–6.

What do we learn about Jehoshaphat's relationship with God?

_____

_____

The power to affect our fears is not something we can do in our own strength. It is the result of a life hidden in Christ. Those who walk with God can walk in the Spirit rather than the flesh. Jehoshaphat did not just give lip service to his faith. He structured his life around obedience to God. Sometimes anxiety strikes us the hardest when we are not spending time with God daily. Jehoshaphat was prepared for unexpected battles because he was truly a follower of God. Religion cannot prepare us, but a relationship with God steadies us for whatever fire we will face.

READ 2 CHRONICLES 20:5–12.

What strikes you about Jehoshaphat's prayer to God? Write down his prayer strategy.

_____

_____

When we are facing fear and anxiety, prayer is the best starting point. Jehoshaphat's prayer reminds me of the A.C.T.S. prayer model (adoration, confession, thanksgiving, and supplication). He began his prayer with adoration of God. He appealed to God's promises, and He asked God for help.

Sometimes when we pray, we give in to anxiety because our prayers are centered on the problem and desire for God's deliverance. But even in the desire for God's rescue, when there is surrender to God's salvation rather than our own attempts to save ourselves, God moves in powerful ways.

Facing our fears with the knowledge that God is all-powerful and already has won helps us view our temporary anxiety in light of eternity. No, our problems do not magically go away, but maybe we can learn to rise above our problems and face them *with* God rather than by ourselves. Use Jehoshaphat's prayer strategy to defeat the spiritual battle of anxiety. Handling spiritual problems in the Spirit works a lot better than trying to battle in the flesh.

Day Four: Setting Your Faith

"So we can confidently say, "The Lord is my helper; I will not fear; what can man do to me?"
Hebrews 13:6 ESV

Just saying we choose faith over fear will not give us the strength we need in the battle over anxiety. But it is a start. Faith needs to be informed by facts, not feelings. Our faith is set when we choose to believe God's thoughts and Word over our own. When we focus on God's promises, not our expectations, we realize that anxiety never could defeat God's promises even if our expectations are not met. God promises to use it all—all that we experience in this messy life—for His glory and our good. I don't know how He does it, but I am living proof He does and His promises never fail. This truth alone helps me to let go of anxiety and its lies—that God cannot handle any problem I face or that God has forgotten me. Setting our faith on the spiritual realities rather than the physical, earthly realities helps us to focus on eternity rather than the temporary present.

READ 2 CHRONICLES 20:20.

_____

_____

Jehoshaphat's pep talk was not just hype. it was solidly based on belief in God and his promises. when we believe in God, we debunk the unbelief that God cannot handle our anxiety. Our faith is set when we choose to worship God through our anxiety rather than choosing to worry.

READ 2 CHRONICLES 20:21.

_____

_____

This does not sound like much of a battle plan to the world. Pray, then worship? Notice that in their worship they are thanking God for what they have not yet received. They are not faking it but banking their fate on God's truth and promises, the spiritual reality rather then the physical one.

Day Five: Restoring Peace

*"You keep him in perfect peace whose mind is
stayed on you, because he trusts in you."*
Isaiah 26:3 ESV

I am amazed when I consider that Jehoshaphat did not just run and hide. The odds were stacked against him, but he looked to another strength other than his own and chose peace through prayer and worship, relying on God's promises rather than his own odds. We get to choose what we fix our minds upon. Jehoshaphat chose to fix his mind on God, not the enemy or the battle that lie ahead. This is supernatural faith, that rises above life's harsh realities. And this grace and supernatural faith is available to us through Christ, today.

READ 2 CHRONICLES 17:3–4.

What was it about Jehoshaphat that enabled him to rise above anxiety?

_____

_____

Jehoshaphat followed the example of a godly father and he sought after God. Sometimes we can call ourselves followers of Jesus, but we might not follow so well. Jehoshaphat did not follow the evil practices in His day or worship anyone or anything but God. And yet if we continue reading Jehoshaphat's story, we see that wealth and success went to his head and he made an alliance with King Ahab, even though he was warned by the prophet Micaiah (2 Chronicles 18). Despite this

Make Up Your Mind (Study Guide)

failure, his foundation of following God is what prepared him for the anxiety he faced in 2 Chronicles 20 when the armies of the Moabites, Ammonites, and some of the Meunites declared war on Jehoshaphat. None of us are perfect followers of God, but when we take our messy lives and surrender them to God, coming back to Him again and again, we can have victory over anxiety or any mindset we face. Following after God is when we immerse ourselves in His Word and way so much that we begin to look like Jesus to those around us.

READ 2 CHRONICLES 22:9.

What does this scripture say about Jehoshaphat's character?

_____

_____

Sometimes we lack peace because we seek peace itself rather than the One Who *is* our peace. Jehoshaphat sought hard after God. Faith informed his actions. We can have perfect peace in Christ. When we doubt this reality, we need to confess and repent of our unbelief. God is able, friends, to give us a perfect peace even when the waves are stirred within and all around us.

READ 2 THESSALONIANS 3:16.

Do you believe God can give you peace at ALL times in EVERY way?

_____

_____

If you are struggling to find the peace that Christ promises, pause and pray right now. Ask God to show you what is robbing you of peace. It might require laying down your idea of peace and picking up the peace of God that rises above our circumstances.

Weekly Wrap-Up

Chapter Three Reflection Questions

Which trigger did you identify with the most?

_____

_____

Which tip is your "go to strategy" when it comes to over-coming an anxious mindset?

_____

_____

How did Christ handle anxiety?

_____

_____

The Keys to Mindset Hacks

Write down the keys from chapter three and any other insight that was significant to you.

Key Thought

_____

_____

Key Verse

_____

_____

Key Change

_____

_____

Counselor's Corner

Battling Anxiety

Mindset Meditation

When anxiety was great within me,
your consolation brought me joy.
Psalm 91:2 (NIV)

After taking some deep breaths and getting in a comfortable position, visualize all the worries that are currently on your heart and mind. Now see yourself laying them at the foot of the cross or on the throne of Heaven.

Take a moment to listen to God's consolation for you. Is He giving you words of comfort, asking you to take a specific action, or encouraging you to let go of the heavy load you've been carrying that He wants you to surrender to Him?

Then soak up His joy. Remind yourself of a promise you've read in the Bible or visualize a moment in time where you sensed His presence so deeply that tears of relief, release and even joy well up in you and out through your eyes.

Record on the lines below what you gave to God and what it felt like to let it go and receive His joy.

_____

_____

_____

_____

Mindset Movement

Write on the lines below a statement using either "even though" or "with God's help."

_____

_____

_____

_____

Questions for Connection

Share with your group what you learned from the Mindset Movements.

1. Share some of the statements you wrote during the Mindset Movement exercise and how using them has reduced your anxiety.
2. Share about a recent or past struggle you've had with feeling anxious.

3. Share a problem in your life that might change if you applied the principle of "with God's help" to it when you thought about it or worked on it.
4. How are you feeding your worry dragon? What could you do differently to start starving it?

Additional Resources

Your Brain Is Always Listening: Tame the Hidden Dragons That Control Your Happiness, Habits, and Hang-Ups by Daniel G. Amen

Breaking Anxiety's Grip: How to Reclaim the Peace God Promises by Dr. Michelle Bengtson

Notes or Questions from Chapter Reading

_____

_____

_____

_____

_____

_____

_____

_____

_____

_____

_____

_____

_____

_____

WEEK FOUR

"When the righteous cry for help, the Lord hears and delivers them out of all their troubles. The Lord is near to the brokenhearted and saves the crushed in spirit."

Psalm 34:17-18 ESV

Chapter 4

The Depressive Mindset— Battling Discouragement and Disillusionment

*"I waited patiently for the Lord; he turned to me
and heard my cry. He lifted me out of the slimy
pit, out of the mud and mire; he set my feet
upon a rock and gave me a firm place to stand.
He put a new song in my mouth,
a hymn of praise to our God."*
Psalm 40:1-3(a) NIV

Life is a gift. But depression can cloud our view of life based on our expectations of it. When we look for hope or happiness from life, rather than looking to the Author of life for hope and joy, we struggle to find satisfaction and can wind up discouraged or worse, depressed. We can remain in bondage to depression when we believe our feelings over our faith; our words over God's. We can fail to recognize that placing confidence in our feelings over God's never-failing promises keeps

78

us trapped in the walls of our mind. Feelings are not fact, but God's Word is true.

Jeremiah saw God's Words were what he needed (Jeremiah 15:16). Do we see that? Doubt creeps in and we give in to despair because we don't believe that God's Word has power and authority over our feelings and our lives. What do we have to lose? When we are depressed, we can do what Jeremiah did. Talk to God about it. Get into His Word. Jeremiah did not play Bible roulette. The Bible says he "ate" God's Word. He was hungry for it and meditated on it until the fog of depression was put into a proper eternal, biblical, godly, and truthful perspective. We can even go on Google and type in a topical search for Scriptures to help with depression. Ask God for the grace to believe His Words above your own feelings. Pray and trust Him to help you. The solution to depression is spiritual. That does not mean medication or counseling cannot be integral parts of our healing. But when we seek healing from God first, we might not need as much intervention from man as we first thought.

Day One: The Trouble with Happiness

"The triumph of the wicked has been
short lived and the joy of the godless
has been only temporary?"
Job 20:5 NLT

Any parent with a toddler knows how hard it is to keep a child happy. The trouble with happiness is that it is temporary and often fickle. One child in poverty can have happiness while one with great riches has none. Circumstances can produce temporary happiness, but they can also easily cause that happiness to vanish as quickly as it first appeared. Sinful man can find happiness, for a while. But for the righteous, there is joy that no earthly temporary happiness can compare. Still, we can miss joy when we search for it rather than abiding in the joy we already have in Christ. Job learned that happiness could not be based on circumstances. This was not just lip service. After he came through the trials of this earth, he understood and looked to God for happiness.

READ JOHN 16:24.

Have you asked God for joy? What does joy mean to you?

_____

_____

Sometimes we can be hesitant to ask God for anything, let alone joy. We are afraid our requests won't be answered. But maybe that is placing hope in God answering in the way we want Him to rather than hoping in God as our joy and solution.

Do you believe God has a joy for you greater than any other joy?

_____

_____

READ JOB 2:10.

Our culture likes to blame God when blessings are removed. What does this verse say about Job's response?

_____

_____

READ PSALM 56:8.

Hagar named God "the God Who sees" (Genesis 16:13). This is the only place in the Bible where this name is recorded. David wrote about God being intimately acquainted and knowing about our suffering. How does God seeing you in your pain comfort you? Does it comfort you?

_____

_____

The trouble with happiness is that we base it on the world's definition. We think a good God should relieve any sorrow or suffering. But he wants to be our comfort in that suffering. He willingly chose suffering for us all.

READ ISAIAH 53:3–5.

How does this prophesy of Jesus' difficult circumstances impact your suffering? Are you willing to view your suffering as a mission from God? Will you be faithful to walk through your suffering as a mission with Jesus?

_____

_____

Suffering can be an impetus for the depressive mindset. Unless we see suffering through a different lens. You are seen in your suffering, friend. And none of your suffering is ever in vain. God redeems our suffering every time for His glory and our good. Christ did not have to suffer mentally, but He chose to. He chose to become the Son of Man to identify with our weaknesses so He could show us the way to victory. He did not give in to the sorrow. We don't have to either.

READ HEBREWS 12:3.

How does considering Christ's suffering impact yours?

_____

_____

The trouble with happiness is in looking to anything other than God for our happiness. Tomorrow we will explore the secret of happiness.

Day Two: The Secret of Happiness

"If they listen and serve Him, they will end their days in prosperity, And their years in happiness."
Job 36:11 NASB

Happiness, then, cannot be based on anything this world offers—not lasting happiness. Elihu, the one comrade of Job's who did not receive rebuke for his counsel to Job knew a secret about happiness. It did not come by hunting for happiness, but simply by obeying and serving God. Perhaps the definition of happiness is part of the problem. We can think prosperity, happiness, and success are words that mean something different than they actually do. Happiness is not an emotion as much as it is a disposition of contentment that no circumstance or emotion can take away. It is embedded in faith in a perfect God, Who is our source of happiness and hope. Hope is the antidote for depression. Just ask Jeremiah. Jeremiah revealed how one can have hope even during great suffering. The hope God promised through Jeremiah was not immediate, but it was a promise. David and Job also showed us how to press into this hope.

READ PSALM 34:8.

How do you taste and see that the LORD is good?

_____

_____

The Psalmist "tasted" and saw that the LORD was good by seeking Him, praising Him, and fearing Him. In short, by being in relationship with Him. The secret to happiness is that it cannot be found by searching for it. It is found in the presence of God.

How does His goodness affect our happiness?

_____

_____

Knowing that our God is good is sweet relief to a sinner's soul. His goodness eclipses and covers our unrighteousness. There is no greater joy!

READ 119:2.

How can a divided heart impede finding happiness?

_____

_____

When we seek God with all our heart, sin does not steal our joy as it does when our hearts are divided.

READ PSALM 86:11

What does an undivided heart help us to do?

_____

_____

A divided heart leads us to fear everything as we are led by our conflicted hearts but an undivided heart leads us to fear God, which conquers all our fears.

READ GALATIANS 5:22–23.

How is joy produced according to Scripture?

_____

_____

READ PSALM 16:11.

Where is joy/happiness found?

_____

_____

The absence of trouble is not where joy is found. The presence of God is. How do you enter God's presence? Do you think God's presence is just for other super spiritual Christians? Or for you?

_____

_____

Day Three: The Definition of Happiness

"Oh, the joys of those who do not follow the advice of the wicked, or stand around with sinners, or join in with mockers."
Psalm 1:1 NLT

In this opening verse and introduction to the Psalms, David pronounces where happiness is _not_ found. By opening the book of Psalms with this word, the stage is set for a book that defines what the blessed happy life is. Happiness is not defined by emotions. It is not defined by circumstances or relationships. Happiness is defined by our Maker, Who designed us to find joy in His presence and in His ways. Trying to find happiness apart from God's definition of happiness will leave us empty. The world around us will try to tempt us to seek happiness from the creation rather than the Creator. But temporary joy only sets us up for greater discouragement when once again our hope for happiness is not able to withstand life's pain. The entire Psalms reveal the struggle for joy and how sin robs us of happiness. Repeatedly David reveals that being in the presence of God and walking with Him is where happiness is found.

READ PSALM 127:5.

Our culture and God's Word provide different definitions of happiness. For example, children are a blessing according to God's Word, but our culture considers them a burden. How do you navigate the lies of our culture that point us to faulty definitions of happiness or discouragement and reorient yourself to God's definition of joy?

_____

_____

READ 1 PETER 1:8

How did Peter find and define joy? Does believing in Jesus help to overcome constantly dwelling on your suffering?

_____

_____

Belief in Jesus eclipses the unbelief germinating within our own minds but we must admit our unbelief in order to access this joy.

Day Four: Depression is More than an Emotion

"My soul has been excluded from peace;
I have forgotten happiness."
Lamentations 3:17 NASB

Jeremiah was being real about the lack of happiness he felt. Discouragement and depression are real, whether brought on by circumstances or inner mental turmoil. Happiness is based on God's promises and God's character. Jeremiah knew this. "But this I call to mind, and therefore I have hope: The steadfast love of the LORD never ceases; his mercies never come to an end; they are new every morning; great is your faithfulness. 'The Lord is my portion,' says my soul, 'therefore I will hope in him'" (Lamentations 3:21-24, ESV). The LORD was his portion. These words are precious to me because, in my darkest moments, they reminded me that God was enough and He is my portion—nothing else will satisfy. We were meant to find our happiness in the Creator, not the creation! His promises are the reality we must cling to when our temporary reality is more than we can bear. But the battle for happiness is excruciatingly difficult when depression is present. We are surrounded by a great cloud of witnesses who encountered depression, but battled through it to find hope, joy, and peace. Ironically, we discover the absence of troubles does not produce joy; troubles lead us to our one, true Joy.

READ PSALM 40:1–2.

Have you faced a season of depression that seemed insurmountable to climb out of? How did you counter those feelings?

_____

_____

We can learn a lot in times of waiting if we wait *with* God. David learned to wait on God by crying out to God, worshiping Him, and trusting in Him. In Lamentations 3:21-24, Jeremiah shows us another strategy. He recalled God's truth and realized that God's Word was the hope that brought lasting happiness; not the absence of troubles. How do you inform your mind when you are tempted to give in to depression? Share a testimony of what God taught you in that place.

_____

_____

Sometimes we feel a need to be "true to our feelings," but our feelings are not true to us. We need to lay down "our truth" before God's truth. How do you examine your emotions in light of what God's Word says?

_____

_____

88

READ PROVERBS 16:32

We don't have to give in to sad feelings. We have a choice: let ourselves be tortured by our emotions or rule them. How do you rule your spirit or emotions?

_____

_____

God has already overcome. We have also. We just need to learn to walk in Christ's victory rather than struggling on our own. David showed us how to overcome time and again.

READ PSALM 42:11.

What did David do to pull himself out of depression?

_____

_____

How do you put your hope in God? Write down some reminders to help you when you need to pull yourself out of the pit of depression.

_____

_____

Day Five: Releasing Expectations

"Beloved, do not be surprised at the fiery ordeal among you, which comes upon you for your testing, as though something strange were happening to you; but to the degree that you share the sufferings of Christ, keep on rejoicing, so that at the revelation of His glory you may also rejoice and be overjoyed."
1 Peter 4:12-13 NASB

We tend to expect a trouble-free life and are shocked when life is hard. This creates disillusionment as our expectations are unmet. Expectations for life and expectations for relationships can leave us broken and depressed. Sometimes this happens because our expectations have become idols that need to be laid down. Peter challenges us to think of our trials differently. We want God's deliverance and salvation to mean that troubles stop. But what if they remain? Can we really rejoice in suffering? Yes. It is a supernatural response available for those who are in Christ who have learned to lay down their expectations for this world and place them in God's capable hands. We were made for eternity and long for perfection (Ecclesiastes 3:11). We have this perfection inside us because of the Holy Spirit. We can tap into His expectations through prayer and God's Word. Let's look at how David's perspective in trials was altered when he considered God's motivation in those trials.

READ PSALM 66:12.

How does this Scripture make you feel? Do you feel betrayed that God allows trials in? Does this cause you to doubt His goodness?

_____

_____

What was God's ultimate goal in the verse above?

_____

_____

READ JOHN 16:33.

We tend to think this earth should be like Heaven. But in light of the troubles Jesus promised us in this world, what should be our response?

_____

_____

READ PSALM 73.

Oftentimes depression comes from our relationships. Expectations in those relationships and the drama, jealousy, striving, and mental head games we torment one another with play a role as well. We should question our thoughts before we ever let an accusation against another brother or sister settle into our Spirit. David learned how to let go of jealousy when wicked people who had harmed him were thriving. What did David realize and when did he realize it?

_____

_____

Friend, can you let go of your plans for your life? Can you trust God with your expectations and view life as a mission that you are on with Christ? God will never let you down. Disillusionment is an illusion. Feelings are illusions, friends. They are works of imagination we can turn into a better reality. Counterfeit joy found in this world is not lasting. Joy is not something we can buy or something we can own. It is something we access as we seek Christ.

Paul reminded us how we access joy by believing God can give it: "May the God of hope fill you with all joy and peace *in believing*, so that by the power of the Holy Spirit you may abound in hope" (Romans 15:13 ESV). Have we asked God to release us from a depressive mindset? Sometimes we have not because we ask not.

Weekly Wrap-Up

Chapter Four Reflection Questions

Which trigger did you identify with the most?

_____

_____

Which tip is your "go to strategy" when it comes to over-coming the depressive mindset?

_____

_____

How did Christ handle depression?

_____

_____

The Keys to Mindset Hacks

Write down the keys from chapter four and any other insight that was significant to you.

Key Thought

_____

_____

Key Verse

_____

_____

Key Change

_____

_____

Counselor's Corner

Battling Depression

Mindset Meditation

*"I remember my affliction and my wandering,
the bitterness and the gall.
I well remember them, and my soul is
downcast within me.
Yet this I call to mind and therefore I have
hope:*

*Because of the LORD'S GREAT LOVE WE ARE NOT
CONSUMED, for his compassions never fail.
They are new every morning; great is your
faithfulness."*
Lamentations 3:19-23 NIV

For this meditation, I encourage you to play worship music in the background because when we take a moment to dwell on things that are creating depression in our lives, we are battling darkness.

Once again, I want you to take some deep breaths and go to a place where you won't be interrupted. I sometimes choose to stay in the car in my driveway before entering my house. Hiding in the car, keeps me at a comfortable temperature. If I have the time, I try to find a place in nature even if it's just a nearby park. When I'm with God in His creation, it allows me to connect with Him quickly.

Now tell yourself and your downcast soul these words by meditating on them repeatedly.

I have hope.
The Lord's love is great.
God has compassion for me and my life.
God's love will never fail me.
God's compassion is new every morning.
God's faithfulness is great.

You might end your time by listening to a hymn or singing a worship song that focuses on God's faithfulness during hard times. If you can't access any music, I've shared some of the lyrics to one of my favorite hymns below. If you prefer more contemporary music, I recommend "The Goodness of God."

Great Is Thy Faithfulness

Great is Thy faithfulness, O God my Father
There is no shadow of turning with Thee
Thou changest not, Thy compassions, they fail not
As Thou hast been, Thou forever will be
Great is Thy faithfulness
Great is Thy faithfulness
Morning by morning new mercies I see
All I have needed Thy hand hath provided
Great is Thy faithfulness, Lord, unto me

Mindset Movement

See Mindset Movement number one in *Make Up Your Mind*. Fold your paper and take the time to write out those negative thoughts on one side of the folded paper and God's truth beside the lies on the other side. Circle one truth you will dwell on this week. Keep coming back to this sheet weekly until you can testify to the freedom you've found for each lie.

On the lines below, write out the truth you chose for this week.

_____

_____

_____

_____

Questions for Connection

1. Share the truth you dwelt on this week from the Mindset Movement exercise above.
2. Share about a time your heart felt sick due to deferred hope. If you are still struggling, ask someone to pray for you. If you are in a group, allow them to pray for you now. If your hope has been restored, share your testimony of the goodness of God.
3. Explain which practical tip has the most potential to lift your spirits this week: writing and posting "I am" statements, exercising, consulting a doctor, or music therapy.

Make Up Your Mind (Study Guide)

4. Share what you learned and think about the difference between the depressive mindset and depression.

Additional Resources

Are You Really OK?: Getting Real About Who You Are, How You're Doing, and Why It Matters by Debra Fileta and Levi Lusko

Bondage Breaker by Neil T. Anderson

Notes or Questions from Chapter Reading

_____

_____

_____

_____

_____

_____

_____

_____

_____

_____

_____

_____

_____

_____

_____

WEEK FIVE

"I am not saying this because I am in need, for I have learned to be content whatever the circumstances."

Philippians 4:11 ESV

The Discontented Mindset—Battling Comparison and Pride

"Don't love money; be satisfied with what you have. For God has said, 'I will never fail you. I will never abandon you.'"
Hebrews 13:5 NLT

We struggle to find satisfaction in a world that was never intended to be our satisfaction. And then that struggle can become idolatry as we bang our heads against the proverbial wall wondering why the created cannot satisfy the longing of our souls. It was never meant to, friend. Pleasure drives us to satisfy the innate fleshly needs we have, but lasting satisfaction is only found in the Spirit, which enables us to be content with whatever this rollercoaster ride called life brings our way. Like Jonah, we can think our view is the one God should adopt. He should acquiesce to what we think is fair or right or good. Given that there is nothing good in us, (Romans 3:10,

Jeremiah 17:9), we cannot possibly know what would truly satisfy and what is right. But Father knows best.

The discontentment from this life is due to our faulty expectations from this life and a lack of gratitude that clutches our hopes and dashes them. Are you tired of repeating the same cycle of riding the ups and downs, friend? We don't have to be numb to this life to have contentment. True contentment does not budge when it is grounded in faith in God's promises. Let's let go of the contentment we pursue and pursue Christ as our satisfaction. We might be surprised that the satisfaction we thought we would never find was there all along.

Day One: The Purpose of Satisfaction

"And the Lord will guide you continually and satisfy your desire in scorched places and make your bones strong; and you shall be like a watered garden, like a spring of water, whose waters do not fail."
Isaiah 58:11 ESV

When we seek satisfaction apart from God, we will never find it . . . sure, maybe temporarily we might think we have, but in a fallen world, there is no lasting satisfaction. God wants to satisfy us with Himself. There is no comparison to that. But like the Israelites, we have often gone to cheap counterfeits hoping they could do the trick. We look for satisfaction in what we own to the point that it sometimes owns us. We look for satisfaction in entertainment so we can temporarily escape the mundanity of life. We look for satisfaction in relationships, expecting people to complete us, when we are already offered completeness in Christ. Our longing souls just want satisfaction that helps us feel like we have enough, where we don't lack for anything. But Scripture says the flesh is never satisfied (Proverbs 27:20). We were meant to hunger, but after the right things.

READ ECCLESIASTES 5:10–11.

Are you satisfied with God's provision in your life? Why or why not?

_____

_____

READ PSALM 63:5.

How are you satisfied by food? Portion? Taste? What is your response to that satisfaction?

_____

_____

Notice that the psalmist showed his satisfaction by praising God. Sometimes we show our satisfaction by craving for more. Is satisfaction a choice? Or how do we determine satisfaction?

_____

_____

READ PROVERBS 13:25.

Why do you think the righteous have enough and the wicked do not?

_____

_____

Determining what is enough is not determined by our craving or by comparison. Our portion will change in different seasons of this life and our level of satisfaction will have to adjust to those changes in provision. The question is whether we can trust God's provision.

READ PSALM 107:9.

Do you believe God satisfies you with good things?

_____

_____

READ PSALM 90:14.

Are you satisfied with your time with God?

_____

_____

If we are not first satisfied with God, nothing will ultimately satisfy us. Are you consistent in your time with God? Why or why not? And how do you think time with God impacts your ability to be content and satisfied with your lot in this life?

_____

_____

READ JEREMIAH 31:25.

Are you weary, friend? Wish you could just be satisfied? God promises to satisfy us. Rest in Him and lay your wants at His feet. Trust Him and watch what He will do. The purpose of our quest for satisfaction is to lead us to the only One who can satisfy. Don't let imposters steal that satisfaction from you. Write a prayer confessing your heart to God and ask Him to help you be satisfied in Him.

_____

_____

_____

_____

Day Two: The Taskmaster of our Wants

"Delight yourself in the Lord, and he will give you the desires of your heart."
Psalm 37:4 ESV

Like an addiction to contentment, we can create many options to satisfy us when we feel bored or discontent. But what then? We think our wants are what we truly want. But before long, we can become enslaved to them and even idolize them. The flesh rears its ugly head when someone does not get their way. When we feel the flesh rising up, demanding its way, we can walk in the Spirit. We might need to get into God's Word and convince our hungry souls that the craving we need satisfied most is in the Spirit. God's provision might not always be what we want, but it is always what we need. If we don't rule our wants, our wants will rule us.

READ ROMANS 14:17.

What is to be our satisfaction?

_____

_____

READ ROMANS 7:15–20.

Where do our wants begin?

_____

_____

READ GALATIANS 5:16.

How can you overcome your wants?

_____

_____

READ ROMANS 8:6–8.

What does giving in to our fleshly desires rather than walking in the Spirit achieve for us?

_____

_____

Following the flesh makes it impossible to please God. That is a hefty consequence. It can be difficult to forge new habits when our mindset has been fixed on doing things according to the flesh. But salvation in Christ gave us the Holy Spirit and we no longer *have* to walk in the flesh. Rather than following the flesh that leads to our destruction, we can rise above to walk in the Spirit as we hunger after God.

READ JOHN 8:36.

Do you walk in this freedom? Why or why not?

_____

_____

God wants to free you from looking to your wants for contentment, friend. He has already completed the work of your salvation and will complete the work of your sanctification as you rely on Him. Admitting our struggle is humbling but frees us to begin to heal.

Day Three: Rewiring Our Contentment

*"But seek first the kingdom of God and his
righteousness, And all these things
will be added to you."*
Matthew 6:33 ESV

Sometimes we might think we know what we want, but we were eternally wired. This is what makes us long for something more. Solomon wrote about this frustration within the human soul. "Yet God has made everything beautiful for its own time. He has planted eternity in the human heart, but even so, people cannot see the whole scope of God's work from beginning to end" (Ecclesiastes 3:11 ESV). Life can leave us feeling jaded, and we can doubt that God has indeed made everything beautiful when we look around and see suffering and affliction. But God never said those things were beautiful. Our contentment wasn't meant to be wired according to the flesh. Instead of seeking our satisfaction, when we rewire our strategy to truly seek God—studying His Word and longing for Him, our satisfaction is transformed.

READ JONAH 4:1–3.

Why do you think Jonah had a problem with God's plan?

_____

_____

READ JONAH 1:9–10.

Did Jonah seem like someone who truly feared God?

_____

_____

READ JONAH 2:1.

How did Jonah rewire his perspective of God's plan?

_____

_____

Even after God worked on Jonah's heart, he shifted back to discontentment when discomfort was allowed in.

READ JONAH 4:6–11.

What do you think about God removing the comfort from Jonah? How do you respond when life gets uncomfortable?

_____

_____

READ MATTHEW 5:6.

What rewiring needs to happen in your life? What is it about God's plan for your life that you have a problem with? How could you reorient your thinking?

_____

_____

We can be tempted to view things from a humanistic perspective rather than a biblical perspective but do so to our own harm. Centering our lives around ourselves and our wants will ultimately make us miserable. The flesh never has enough. God is still good even if we doubt His goodness. His purposes still stand even if we do not cooperate. When we stop fighting God's plan, we find the contentment He wanted us to have all along.

Day Four: The Greatest Gain

"Now there is great gain in godliness with contentment."
1 Timothy 6:6 ESV

Do you wonder what Jonah really wanted? What would have been the greatest gain for him and brought him the greatest satisfaction? It seems he wanted the Ninevites to be decimated. Kind of like the imprecatory psalms David wrote when he asked God to get the bad guys. It makes sense. Makes things "even." The Ninevites were cruel enemies of God's people. Wouldn't God be on the Israelites' side? His own people? But God had a bigger, greater gain and plan--the salvation of even our enemies. His plans are always redemptive and good. What if God gave in to what would satisfy Jonah's sense of justice? Judgment without hope. Ultimately the Ninevites would revert from their repentance experienced in the days of Jonah and be judged by God in the future, but that was many years after Jonah. Can we trust God's hand and plan when they don't match ours, knowing His thoughts are higher than ours? The greatest gain we will ever find in this world is what God has for us.

READ PHILIPPIANS 3:7–8.

The kingdom of God is a major paradigm shift. It is other worldly. Supernatural. But it is accessible to those who are "in" Christ. Paul had a major turnaround, and so can we. What do you think Paul realized that changed his perspective?

_____

_____

READ 1 CORINTHIANS 2:9–10.

Paul saw it. Do we? It can be hard to see the spiritual realities all around us when the physical realities are so loud. Seeing the spiritual reality as greater than the temporary reality requires faith and letting go of what we thought was a greater gain. Share what deep things God has shown you that helped you see past temporary things through an eternal lens?

_____

_____

Day Five: The Cost of Discontentment

"'Arise, go to Nineveh, the great city, and cry out against it, because their wickedness has come up before Me.' But Jonah got up to flee to Tarshish from the presence of the Lord."
Jonah 1:1-3a NASB

Pass & Nietert

The purpose of this life is not satisfaction. It is knowing and worshiping God. It is being used by Him to help others know Him. When we are not grateful for our lot in this life, it can cause us to miss God's will. When we are discontent, we can't be sent. This is a high cost that we don't want to pay. But there are other costs to discontentment. Those around us are impacted. Relationships are harmed while we compare and succumb to jealousy and pride because of our lack of contentment with God's portion for us.

READ PHILIPPIANS 2:3.

Rather than comparing to others and minimizing them in our eyes to inflate ourselves or try to feel more content in this life, what does Paul instruct us to do?

_____

_____

The supernatural life of walking in the Spirit helps us to rejoice when others succeed. Their success is not something to be compared to. It is something to celebrate and to praise God for. Sacrifice brings greater joy than scrambling to get our share.

READ PROVERBS 11:2.

. When we release jealousy, pride, and the strivings of man in our effort to find the contentment we think we lack, we finally escape the rat race of the pursuit to always be better than the Jones'. What ironically comes with pride?

_____

_____

READ ROMANS 12:2.

What needs to happen for us to recognize what is actually good and right; what will satisfy us?

_____

_____

Sacrifice brings greater joy than scrambling to get our share. The cost of discontentment is high. It robs our relationships, our mindset, and our effectiveness for the Gospel, which impacts all eternity. Being satisfied in Christ is one of the great witnesses the world so desperately needs to see.

Weekly Wrap-Up

Chapter Five Reflection Questions

Which trigger did you identify with the most?

_____

_____

Which tip is your "go to strategy" when it comes to over-coming the discontent negative mindset?

_____

_____

How did Christ handle discontentment?

_____

_____

The Keys to Mindset Hacks

Write down the keys from chapter five and any other insight that was significant to you.

Key Thought

_____

_____

Key Verse

_____

_____

Key Change

_____

_____

Counselor's Corner

Battling Discontent

Mindset Meditation

*Therefore, since we are surrounded by such
a great cloud of witnesses, let us throw off
everything that hinders and the sin that
so easily entangles. And let us run with
perseverance the race marked out for us.*
Hebrews 12:1 NIV

Are you ready to race? Don't worry, today's meditation exercise doesn't involve tennis shoes or sweating. Instead, in a comfortable position while breathing deeply, visualize yourself running in the race of life on God's Kingdom team.

First, see your cloud of witnesses. These are the people who cheer you on. Next, pray through any heavy baggage, sin, or pain you've been carrying. Ask God to remove those burdens. This may be all you need to do, or He may show some work to be done with a group, pastor, or counselor.

Now get ready to run. How are you dressed? Maybe with some or all of the armor of God (Eph. 6:10-18). Now see yourself smoothly moving forward, avoiding your life obstacles and temptations. See yourself persevering through injuries and other setbacks and keep on moving.

Finally, remember this is YOUR race. Set an intention from the very start not to get distracted by others whose race might look better to you or whose lane seems easier. Their race is their race, and your race is yours. Looking around will only slow you down.

Mindset Movement

Use the lines below to write out a prayer committing to God and yourself to stay in your own lane. You might also want to ask one friend to help you with this when you are tempted to desire the highlight reel of another person's life.

_____

_____

_____

_____

Questions for Connection

1. Share about your struggles with staying in your own lane and how you will reset your mindset when you are tempted to compare.
2. How has the comparison game tripped you up in the past?

3. Share something worth celebrating in your current life. Practicing gratitude is a great mindset reset for running your own race with perseverance.

4. Whose success could you genuinely celebrate today? Celebrating life moments with those we love decreases discontent.

Additional Resources

Try Softer: A Fresh Approach to Move Us out of Anxiety, Stress, and Survival Mode—and Into a Life of Connection and Joy by Aundi Kolber

Comparison Girl: Lessons from Jesus on Me-Free Living in a Measure-Up World by Shannon Popkin

Notes or Questions from Chapter Reading

_____

_____

_____

_____

_____

_____

_____

_____

_____

_____

_____

_____

_____

_____

WEEK SIX

"But let him ask in faith, with no doubting, for the one who doubts is like a wave of the sea that is driven and tossed by the wind."

James 1:6 ESV

Chapter 6

The Doubtful Mindset— Battling Unbelief and Hopelessness

*"I certainly believed that I would see the
goodness of the Lord in the land of the living.
Wait for the Lord; be strong and let your heart
take courage; yes, wait for the Lord."*
Psalm 27:13–14 NASB

These words from the psalmist have ministered to my soul many times when my hope failed. The NASB 95 translation renders verse 13 as "I would have despaired if I had not believed." Despair rises when hopes sink into unbelief. Sometimes we think having our hopes fulfilled will be what finally erases all doubts. But behind every hope lingers doubt and a fear that our hopes will not come to fruition. This is when we realize our hopes are not "the" hope we are supposed to have! Laying down our hopes will require dying to self and living for Christ's hope.

Doubts emanate from a heart that has maybe been wounded or jaded by what "should have been." We don't dare to believe again because we just can't risk the hurt. But looking through the lens of "less" will never bring us the "more" we are hoping for. In our struggle to believe that God is enough, we can try to fill our doubts with finding other mechanisms to fill our lack. Converting a doubtful mindset is not just about being positive. It is a transformation of our souls and a recalibration of what we were supposed to be hoping for in the first place. This transformation will require repenting of our unbelief in order to access the faith we need.

Day One: Doubt the Doubts

"Jesus immediately reached out his hand and took hold of him, saying to him, 'O you of little faith, why did you doubt?'"
Matthew 14:31 ESV

Doubts seem so right. They are our own innate thoughts, our truth. But when our own hearts are deceptive (Jeremiah 17:5), we should doubt the doubts, not reinforce them by believing in them. Poor Thomas has been dubbed doubting Thomas because of his need to see before he believed. Jesus resolved his doubts and can resolve ours, too.

READ JOHN 20:24–25.

Thomas did not initially get to see what the disciples saw. But then we haven't either. Why do you think Thomas needed to see and touch the wounds?

_____

_____

Thomas' doubting was of the resurrection. But this was not his first experience with a resurrection.

READ JOHN 11:16.

Following Lazarus' death, Thomas makes an interesting statement. What do you think he meant?

_____

_____

Theologians tend to view Thomas' statement as both an act of bravery as well as resigning himself to what would ultimately be his end. Death is a grim reality. To a doubter, resurrection seems impossible, but to a believer, Christ's resurrection takes the sting out of death. Thomas teetered between being a doubter and a believer. How about us? Are there things we do not understand about Christianity? How do we handle our misunderstanding?

_____

_____

READ JOHN 14:5.

Why do you think Thomas asked this question?

_____

_____

Thomas wasn't doubting Jesus when he asked this question. I believe he genuinely just did not get what "the way" was.

READ JOHN 14:6–7.

What did Jesus point Thomas to in his doubt?

_____

_____

Our doubts focus on what we can understand, on our belief system. Our way is not *the* way though. Jesus is the way. Doubts focus on the wrong thing. As we try to figure out our doubts, we should deny them and point them to Jesus and His Word. Thomas' doubts have likely been ours at some point. Thomas did not know where Jesus was leading (John 14:5). He did not believe Jesus could be raised from the dead (John 20:24-25), and he did not understand what Jesus was about to do in the case of Lazarus. He just did not get it. Until he made Jesus Lord.

READ JOHN 20:27–28.

What is Thomas' statement an indicator of?

_____

_____

Thomas broke through his unbelief by seeing, but not just seeing—taking action on that sight. He professed Jesus as Lord and God. When we doubt Scripture or doubt God, it is His lordship in our lives and placing our faith in Him, no matter what, that shatters our doubt.

READ JOHN 20:29.

What do you lean on for belief when doubt clouds your vision?

_____

_____

Tomorrow we will look at one of the things we tend to rely on for faith that can lead us astray.

Day Two: Foolish Faith

"For the word of the cross is folly to those who are perishing, but to us who are being saved it is the power of God."
1 Corinthians 1:18 ESV

No one wants to be duped. We would rather doubt than foolishly believe in something that does not come to pass. I remember people telling me my faith was a crutch. They did not see their need for faith and preferred to rely on their own strength rather than trust in someone else's ideas, especially God's. But we who are saved know differently. The battle of the mind can cause confusion, but our doubts are extinguished by choosing faith over our doubts.

READ 1 CORINTHIANS 1:21.

What is the fruit of believing?

_____

_____

The fruit of doubt and unbelief is that people will not be saved. Doubting does not help us one bit. Let it go. Trusting in Jesus rescues our souls and our mindsets.

READ ROMANS 10:17.

Where can we find faith when the voices around us are so loud?

_____

_____

READ 2 CORINTHINIANS 5:7.

Why do you think we tend to rely on our senses for faith?

_____

_____

Our senses and emotions are barometers of the flesh. But God can heal our faith meter and show us how to have faith through the Spirit. We will learn about that tomorrow.

Day Three: Healing Doubters

"And have mercy on those who doubt."
Jude 1:22 ESV

We were all doubters, unbelievers, and enemies of the cross once. The brokenness of this world caused us to doubt God's goodness. Our hearts were hurt that God did not seem to care about our suffering. When God heals our doubt, we need to remember to not judge others who still doubt. Their doubt comes from a deep place that needs grace applied.

READ PROVERBS 3:5–8.

Doubts lead to stress that can impact our health. What restores our health?

_____

_____

Our spiritual health and faith are healed not simply by saying we should not doubt, but by choosing to trust the only trustworthy One. Fearing God turns us away from the evil of unbelief.

READ LUKE 24:38.

How does the fact that those closest to Jesus also struggled with doubt impact you?

_____

_____

READ PSALM 77:11–12.

How does thinking on what God has done in the past and what He will do in the future cure your doubts?

_____

_____

Thinking on the works of God informs our faith rather than letting our doubts inform us. Tomorrow we will look at the role that hope places in stopping our doubts.

Day Four: Hoping in the Unseen

"Now faith is the assurance of things hoped for, the conviction of things not seen."
Hebrews 11:1 ESV

It does not take faith to look at the signs of a storm and believe a storm is coming. When the wind starts to blow and the sky darkens, we will likely not just glibly blow off such signs. But just as the wind blows the trees signaling to us that it is there, faith operates in the same manner. We see evidence of God all around us. We see His power in Scripture. We don't have to let a chaotic world create doubt about God still being in control. Faith does not need proof, yet proof is evident all around us.

READ HEBREWS 11:3.

Do you believe God created *the* world? How does this help you to trust Him with *your* world?

_____

_____

READ HEBREWS 11:6.

Do you believe God exists? How does this belief inform your doubt that He can help you?

_____

_____

READ HEBREWS 11:39–40.

If the ancients had faith yet did not receive what they hoped for on this earth, how does that inform our faith? Is your faith only viable as long as you can see what you hope for?

_____

_____

Hope is not hope if it has to be realized in order to be held. Our hope is not in hope itself, but in God Whose character and promises are perfect.

Day Five: Why Did You Doubt?

"Jesus immediately reached out his hand and took hold of him, saying to him, "O you of little faith, why did you doubt?"
Matthew 14:31 ESV

I love that Peter dared to exercise faith. And I completely get it that he had his doubts. We would not be human if we did not struggle to have faith. Still, Jesus' question to Peter in Matthew 14:31 is such a good, introspective question. It is helpful for us to understand where our doubt comes from. And when Peter asked Jesus to help, I love that Scripture says Jesus immediately reached out His hand. When we doubt, we just need to ask for help. God can help our unbelief.

READ MATTHEW 14:30.

What was Peter looking at when doubt overcame him?

_____

_____

READ MATTHEW 26:69–70

What was Peter listening to when he gave in to doubt?

_____

_____

READ MATTHEW 26:35.

What was Peter's bravery based on?

_____

_____

Relying on our senses or on our own reasoning will plunge us into doubt every time. But there is a way out.

READ MARK 9:23–24.

What broke through the father's doubts?

_____

_____

Repentance breaks the shackles of our unbelief. When we ask God to help us with our unbelief He always answers. What doubt do you need to lay aside today? Write out a prayer to God to help you identify and release your unbelief and doubts. Then put on faith.

_____

_____

_____

_____

Weekly Wrap-Up

Chapter Six Reflection Questions

Which trigger did you identify with the most?

_____

_____

Which tip is your "go to strategy" when it comes to overcoming the doubtful mindset?

_____

_____

How did Christ handle doubts?

_____

_____

The Keys to Mindset Hacks

Write down the keys from chapter six and any other insight that was significant to you.

Key Thought

_____

_____

Key Verse

_____

_____

Key Change

_____

_____

Counselor's Corner

Battling Self Doubt & Hopelessness

Mindset Meditation

> *"No, in all these things we are more than conquerors through him who loved us."*
> Romans 8:37 NIV

What do you need to conquer? This week's meditation involves inviting God to join us in our daily battles.

After you take some deep breaths, squeeze each muscle group in your body and release it one at a time, starting at your toes moving up toward your head. You can look up progressive muscle relaxation if you want to learn more about this process.

With your body relaxed, bring THAT battle to mind. You know the one to which I'm referring. The one that keeps returning. It could be about your temper, weight, insecurity, shyness or whatever you've wrestled with for years or maybe even decades.

In your mind, see Jesus taking victory over your struggle while you watch. Then see yourself joining with Him and living differently today, tomorrow and in the days ahead. Spend some time seeing yourself wrestle but make a different choice not because of your own strength but because the power of God is at work within you.

Record your Mindset Meditation experience on the lines below.

_____

_____

_____

_____

Mindset Movement

Write on the lines below some of the promises of God you recorded on your sticky notes and where you placed them.

_____

_____

_____

_____

Questions for Connection

1. Share the promises you wrote for your Mindset Movement and where you placed your sticky notes.
2. How has doubt (self-doubt or hopelessness) kept you at a standstill in the past?
3. Share any rooms in your home that display Scripture on the wall and what led you to choose that verse. Which rooms in your home would be a greater blessing to you with a display of Scripture or Christian art in them and what verses or images would you like to find?
4. What action step will you take this week to restart or propel your momentum?

Additional Resources

Transforming Your Thought Life: Christian Meditation in Focus by Sarah Geringer

Winning the War in Your Mind: Change Your Thinking, Change Your Life by Craig Groeschel

Notes or Questions from Chapter Reading

_____

_____

_____

_____

_____

_____

_____

_____

_____

_____

_____

_____

_____

_____

_____

_____

_____

WEEK SEVEN

"No, in all these things we are more than conquerors through him who loved us."

Romans 8:37 (ESV)

Chapter 7

The Helpless Mindset— Battling Apathy and Weakness

"Likewise the Spirit helps us in our weakness. For we do not know what to pray for as we ought, but the Spirit himself intercedes for us with groanings too deep for words. And he who searches hearts knows what is the mind of the Spirit, because the Spirit intercedes for the saints according to the will of God."
Romans 8:26-27 ESV

Standing on the chair, I groaned with an exasperated tone while I tried to figure out how to change the lightbulb of a complicated light fixture. "Good grief! You'd think there was gold in here as hard as they make it to access that lightbulb!" And I wept in a broken pitiful whimper. Small things become huge when we are surrounded by problems. I was in the middle of one of the hardest seasons of my life and it seemed like I could not catch a break. Everything tends to break at the same time when we go through traumatic events. Why does everything have to be so hard? Have you ever asked that question? Cars break down. Relationships, too. This broken world breaks everything down over time. But God.

I think people who knew me in that particular season of my life would probably have thought my situation looked a bit helpless, too, but they also knew my God was not. Sometimes in our helplessness we can want to give up and resort to apathy or weakness. But our helplessness becomes a place of strength when we stop relying on faulty security and rely on God instead.

Day One: When it is All Too Much

"For we do not have a high priest who is unable to sympathize with our weaknesses, but one who in every respect has been tempted as we are, yet without sin."
Hebrews 4:15 ESV

How does it make you feel to know you have a High Priest who is sympathetic? Sometimes when we are overcome in this life, people tell us to pull up our big girl pants. But Jesus understands. He subjected Himself to our weaknesses, but He did not sin. Think about that. He chose to come in weakness to rescue us. This is so counter our idea of strength, isn't it? He is able to help when it seems there is no help.

READ ROMANS 8:26–27.

Have you ever just had groans you could mutter when life seems to be too much? How does the mind of the Spirit help us at such times?

_____

_____

Being overwhelmed happens easily enough. Let's be real—Life is hard. So while we can feel a pressure to "man up" and act like life's troubles are no big deal, admitting when we feel helpless is actually what can begin to bring relief.

READ 1 CORINTHIANS 10:13.

When you are tempted to be frazzled and give into helplessness, what escape does God provide?

_____

_____

Sometimes we can be tempted to not take the way out that God is providing. We might not like His rescue. Or we might doubt that His way out is effective. But God's promises never fail and they are for us all.

READ ROMANS 10:13.

Does God help some or all who ask for His help?

_____

_____

READ ROMANS 5:6.

What was our condition when Christ came to help us?

_____

_____

We can forget the state we were in when God saved us. Sometimes it is helpful to look back and see how utterly helpless we were. Tomorrow we will look at a surprising source of strength that only comes as we admit our helplessness.

Day Two: The Helpless Mission

> *"For the sake of Christ, then, I am content with weaknesses, insults, hardships, persecutions, And calamities. For when I am weak, then I am strong."*
> 2 Corinthians 12:10 ESV

We tend to think being strong is where it is at. Being helpless is not. But perhaps helplessness is not weakness after all. What if our helplessness is what ultimately points us to the greatest strength of all—our salvation. Our helplessness is a mission if we will let it be. Rather than throwing up our arms

Make Up Your Mind (Study Guide)

and wanting out of our helplessness, right there in the middle of our languishing over not being able to fix ourselves, is a surprise we would not have found had we never seen our need.

READ HEBREWS 12:3.

How does considering the seeming helplessness of Christ's suffering help us in our weakness?

_____

_____

When we consider what Christ accomplished, the salvation of the entire world, we know His suffering was worth it. But when we are in the midst of our own suffering, it is hard for us to see the bigger picture. We need to have in front of us a greater hope than merely surviving our suffering.

READ HEBREWS 12:2.

What helped Jesus push through His suffering?

_____

_____

Jesus' joy was fixed on His goal, and as we fix our eyes on Jesus and the unfailing promises of God, we remove the focus from our problems and push through our own suffering.

READ 1 CORINTHIANS 1:27.

Do you think God calls the qualified? Why does He often use weak people?

_____

_____

In times of suffering, we can feel especially vulnerable and weak. But that does not disqualify us; in fact our weakness positions us for God's grace if we acknowledge our need and cry out to Him. In Christ no helplessness is beyond God's aid and no suffering is ever wasted. Tomorrow let's look at a familiar lie that is often behind our helplessness.

Day Three: The Lie of Helplessness

"For a wide door for effective work has opened to me, and there are many adversaries."
1 Corinthians 16:9 ESV

Sometimes we may feel helpless because of a false belief that once we are in Christ, everything will be unicorns and roses. Not so, my friend. Ask Paul. He was constantly dealing with weaknesses, insults, and hardships. But perhaps there is another lie. We always were helpless. We never were enough. Our culture likes to bolster our sense of self-worth, but truly, we were worthless and helpless until Jesus. Isn't that freeing? We never could be enough, so whatever mountain of helplessness we are facing right now, Jesus can handle that, too.

Make Up Your Mind (Study Guide)

READ PHILIPPIANS 4:13.

How do you apply Christ's strength to your life?

_____

_____

Christ's strength is ours for the asking. We tend to think our strength is external, but the outside is a picture of what transpires internally. Our inner being is where our greatest strength lies.

READ EPHESIANS 3:16–19.

What does this power look like in our inner being?

_____

_____

When we feel helpless, our inner being should not be the last resort, but the first. Our resolve and faith are strengthened when we stop trying in our own fleshly strength and stop looking at the waves around us. As we pray to God it is then that we access the power God gives us from his great riches. No, this life is not perfect once we are in Christ, but our Savior is perfect and He has not left us alone.

Day Four: Finding Strength

"For I, the Lord your God, hold your right hand;
it is I who say to you,
'Fear not, I am the one who helps you.'"
Isaiah 41:13 ESV

My tendency in the flesh is to try and figure things out on my own. I must remind myself to ask God for help. He promises to give us wisdom, but somehow, I like to make it difficult on myself and struggle in my helplessness first. Anyone relate? Maybe underneath this self-reliance is unbelief about God's willingness to help. Or perhaps I think His method of helping should look different. Understanding and renouncing what keeps us bound in a helpless mindset helps us break free when we finally run into the arms of Jesus and admit our need.

READ PSALM 46:1–3.

Do you go to God first when trouble strikes? Why do you think we don't run to God first when we feel helpless?

_____

_____

READ JOHN 14:26.

Sometimes we would rather drift from a helpless mindset to a victim one. We might not want the help we say we do. Or we would rather just have God remove us from it. But how can the Holy Spirit help us at such times?

_____

_____

READ JUDE 1:24.

God is able, friend. We are not. Write about how He has shown you recently that He is able.

_____

_____

Day Five: Choosing Strength

"But he said to me, 'My grace is sufficient for you, for my power is made perfect in weakness.' Therefore I will boast all the more gladly of my weaknesses, so that the power of Christ may rest upon me."
2 Corinthians 12:9 ESV

Abigail is such an example of someone who could have been filled with terror but chose strength instead. She did not give into the helpless mindset and funneled that adrenaline into action. She thought about a solution, not the problem (1 Samuel 25:17). She acted on that solution rather than just hoping someone else would rescue her (1 Samuel 25:18). She was brave. Bold. Yet humble. She sided with faith rather than fear. Sometimes we will go through threats in this life that seem bigger than we can handle. When we cooperate with God by doing our part and trusting Him to do His, we have victory. The question is whether we will access this strength or shrink back in unbelief, thinking we are unable to choose the strength God provides?

READ GALATIANS 6:9.

How does being diligent offer us hope when we feel we have no strength?

_____

_____

The law of reaping what we sow provides hope we will reap a harvest if we will just be faithful to do things God's way.

READ PSALM 55:1–3, 16–17.

How can you cast your burden of helplessness on God?

_____

_____

Notice that the psalmist acknowledged he was distraught in his thoughts. Sure, there was external pressure, but his thoughts were what he needed to apprehend.

READ ISAIAH 63:8–9.

How does knowing God is compassionate toward your suffering help you in your suffering?

_____

_____

In what area of your life do you need to choose strength? Everyone is helpless before Jesus. Everyone will encounter troubles in this life, but God always longs to bring us to a place of abundance (Psalm 66:12) and to restore us. Share where you feel helpless below and try to find a Scripture to meet that need.

_____

_____

READ PSALM 71:20–21.

What is God's ultimate goal for us?

_____

_____

God's desire is always to redeem and restore His people. Isn't this good news? Knowing God's heart, holy motivations, perfect character, goodness, and power assures us He is fully able to help us, and He wants to as well. Can we trust Him with *how* He helps? He sees the big picture and His goal is restoration for you. You are loved, friend.

Weekly Wrap-Up

Chapter Seven Reflection Questions

Which trigger did you identify with the most?

_____

_____

Which tip is your "go to strategy" when it comes to over-coming the helpless mindset?

_____

_____

How did Christ handle helplessness?

_____

_____

The Keys to Mindset Hacks

Write down the keys from chapter seven and any other insight that was significant to you.

Key Thought

_____

_____

Key Verse

_____

_____

Key Change

_____

_____

Counselor's Corner

Battling Helplessness

Mindset Meditation

> *"I am the vine; you are the branches. If you remain in me and I in you, you will bear much fruit; apart from me you can do nothing."*
> John 15:5 NIV

As you meditate on this verse, picture yourself as a branch, completely dependent on God as the source of all you need. I love meditating on the words "remain in me" and "bear much fruit" as I lay on my back on a mat on the floor with my arms and legs slightly spread in a comfortable position. I place my hands open and upward so that they may receive and allow the Holy Spirit to flow in and through me.

Stay in this place meditating on these words as long as you are able. If your brain wanders, and it most likely will, just bring your mind back to the verse, taking a few more deep breaths.

Training your brain, body and spirit takes time. When speaking, I often use the metaphor of plugging into the power of God. In our fast-paced lives, stillness and solitude are usually the most challenging and yet most effective ways to tap into God's supernatural power that alone can empower us to overcome feelings of hopelessness.

On the lines below, record the date, how long you spent "remaining in Christ," and any insights Holy Spirit brought to your mind during you time of solitude and stillness.

_____

_____

_____

_____

Mindset Movement

Write out your SMART goal that you worked on this week on the lines below. You might fill in these blanks if you are having trouble completing this exercise.

I will _____ *(action) in or at* _____

(location where you will perform this action) for _____

(amount of time) at _____ *(time of day)*

_____ *number of times this week.*

_____

_____

_____

Questions for Connection

1. Share your SMART goal.
2. In which circumstance might you benefit from having an accountability partner? Whom might you choose?
3. What negative mindset like the ones on page 161 do you need to practice refuting?
4. What practical steps will you take to overcome feelings of helplessness this coming week?

Additional Resources

Attached to God: A Practical Guide to Deeper Spiritual Experience by Krispin Mayfield

Secrets of the Vine: Breaking Through to Abundance by Bruce Wilkinson

Notes or Questions from Chapter Reading

_____

_____

_____

_____

_____

_____

_____

_____

_____

_____

_____

_____

_____

_____

_____

WEEK EIGHT

"Take my yoke upon you, and learn from me, for I am gentle and lowly in heart, and you will find rest for your souls."

Matthew 11:29 ESV

Chapter 8

The Hurried Mindset— Battling Overcommitment and Margin

*"Desire without knowledge is not good,
and whoever makes haste with his
feet misses his way."*
Proverbs 19:2 ESV

Ok, this mindset has been one of my "biggies" and I did not even know it. When a mindset helps us achieve a lot, we can chalk it up to personality and rationalize that it is ok. We do this with all the mindsets though, right? If we are anxious, we blame it on the environment. If we are depressed, we might be able to blame it on our circumstances. But casting blame does not heal our minds, and we have learned that while there are triggers that make maintaining our mindsets challenging, we don't have to give in to the triggers. We can choose the mind of Christ through the tips and Scriptures in the book, *Make Up Your Mind*.

"Hurry Sickness" is what many are calling the Hurried Mindset. Everyone is in a rush these days, right? Stressed out from being over committed in a world that never sleeps, the culture has definitely helped shape the Hurried Mindset in many, but we can learn to push back. We can set goals and have boundaries to help us build in margin. For me, this looks like shutting off my computer when I have planned to, so I am completely present with loved ones. It means bringing my phone on a walk or an outing for emergency purposes but keeping it in my pocket.

Why do we need to deal with this mindset? Hurry can lead to worry and wasted energy. It can be a taskmaster that causes us to be enslaved to schedules rather than breathing the fresh air and enjoying the company of others around us. I have learned that I need to be intentional with my time and let go of what doesn't get done, because my "to do" lists are truly never fully done. You won't regret not having worked more, but you might regret the people you miss by working too much. Grab a cup of tea or coffee and rest while you do this study, friend. No need to rush. And no need to answer every question. Just breathe, pray, and ask the Holy Spirit to lead you.

Day One: Finding Rest

"Desire without knowledge is not good,
and whoever makes haste with his
feet misses his way."
Proverbs 19:2 ESV

Make Up Your Mind (Study Guide)

Today women have a burden upon themselves to be superwoman. If it isn't the Proverbs 31 quotation that makes us all feel inferior, (and that passage is not just one woman, but a poem of many), it is the expectations in our own minds, fanned into flame by comparison and maybe the expectations of others, too. But haste makes waste. We read about what the hurried mindset does in the book, *Make Up Your Mind*, but somehow, we might not be convinced. We struggle to accomplish things in our overcommitted lives and can miss the rest that God provides.

READ MARK 2:27.

Do you find it difficult to rest?

_____

_____

I love how Jesus points out that we were not just made for the Sabbath. Life in Christ is not just about rules. God cares for us. He wants us to be able to rest.

READ HEBREWS 4:9–11.

What is the Sabbath rest for us today? How does this impact a hurried mindset?

_____

_____

READ HEBREWS 4:3.

What role does belief have to do with our ability to rest in God's finished work?

_____

_____

Rest that the writer of Hebrews is telling us about is salvation. God wants us to look at our hearts, not just external measures of rest. Good works will not achieve this rest. When we operate from this framework of rest in Jesus, we don't need to strive to try and prove ourselves. There is time to do God's will. We don't need to rush to do His work.

READ LUKE 10:40.

Can you relate to Martha's stressing out about Mary's resting?

_____

_____

My children were sure to point out if one of their siblings was not doing "their fair share." What is it about work that makes us want to ensure others are doing work, too? The flesh avoids work but we were made to work and work has its place. Martha's work became a distraction. Does your work become a distraction? Why or Why not?

_____

_____

Day Two: Unrest

"Making the best use of the time,
because the days are evil."
Ephesians 5:16 ESV

Underneath our hurrying and scurrying is unrest. This place of tension drives us on a quest that we might not even realize we are on. What if our busyness is incurring the loss of the peace Christ came to bring us? Peeking into the reason for this unrest can help us to stop letting unrest drive us.

READ PROVERBS 28:20.

What was the motivation behind hurrying in this verse and what was the consequence?

_____

_____

Hurrying leads to trouble. Sometimes finances can be an impetus for our busy lives. Our wants exceed God's provision and we become bound to schedules to provide for those wants.

READ PROVERBS 22:7.

Are financial decisions driving your busyness?

_____

_____

READ GALATIANS 1:10.

Sometimes we live our lives in front of an audience in our mind. We strive and are ruled by busyness because we just want to measure up. Does seeking man's approval drive your unrest?

_____

_____

READ JAMES 5:7–8.

Sometimes we are hurried because we just want to see results. What is more important than achieving our goal?

_____

_____

Patience is not a popular word. But patience establishes us more than rushing around does. I love the ESV rendering at the end of James 5:8, "establish your hearts, for the coming of the Lord is at hand." More important than achieving our goals is the character developed during the pursuit of God-given goals. We tend to be focused on the outcome, but God looks at our hearts. The more time we spend cultivating our hearts in God's Word daily, the less hurried we will feel.

Make Up Your Mind (Study Guide)

Day Three: Going Slow

*"But do not overlook this one fact, beloved, that
with the Lord one day is as a thousand years, and
a thousand years as one day. The Lord is not slow
to fulfill his promise as some count slowness, but
is patient toward you, not wishing that any should
perish, but that all should reach repentance."*
2 Peter 3:8-9 ESV

Sunday mornings can reveal what a hurried mindset can do. I have had the tendency to leave just enough time to get ready. I want as much rest as I can get. I realized one day that this was like planning to be hurried. And it created a lot of stress on a Sunday morning. I noticed on one particular Sunday morning that my husband was NEVER rushed on a Sunday morning, or anytime. And honestly, this bugged me. "Hustle!" I quipped when we needed to get into the church building for worship practice. He just smiled at me. I realized in that moment that I was the problem, not him. I still have issues with this, y'all, but I am aware of it and learning to build margin rather than planning to be hurried. And maybe I am learning that it is ok to just go slow.

READ PROVERBS 16:9.

How does God directing your steps impact the need to rush?

_____

_____

I liken our steps to a hamster running on a wheel while God holds the wheel. There is something to be said about being diligent, but also in relying on God's timing and not our own.

READ ECCLESIASTES 3:1.

Sometimes our self-imposed deadlines could have a little more wiggle room. How does knowing there is a time for everything affect your pace in this life?

_____

_____

I have had to tell myself it is ok if my "to do" list takes longer to complete. And _our_ time? God holds it all in His hands, and His plans and timing are beautiful.

READ ECCLESIASTES 3:11.

Perhaps timing isn't the focus, but what God is doing in that time is. Viewing our present demands in light of eternity, how urgent do those demands feel?

_____

_____

READ HABAKKUK 2:2–3.

How does knowing that God's plan and purposes will unfold in _His_ perfect timing impact your timing?

_____

_____

Going slow does not mean we don't press toward our God-given goals. It means we make space for them, but don't feel rushed in the completion of them. This does not mean we are apathetic or lazy. We still need to be diligent, working alongside God. Sometimes there will be busy seasons, but our mindset does not have to be busy. God gives us supernatural grace to accomplish His work. We don't have to stress or be hurried about it. Tomorrow we will look at the role that simplicity plays in our level of stress and hurriedness.

Day Four: Simplicity

"Let us therefore strive to enter that rest, so that
no one may fall by the same
sort of disobedience."
Hebrews 4:11 ESV

There is something comforting about routine. It isn't rushed or demanding when we set it up well. But when we let the world or others establish our routine, we are driven to a state of being hurried. I have had seasons when I had a routine where I would rise super early to seek Jesus because there was no sound or distraction to cause me to hurry through that time. My mind was marked by peace in those seasons. And I have had seasons where I would cram in my time with Jesus. Those seasons provoked a hurried mindset. Simplifying my schedule has helped me make sure my "big rock" is in place first before I crowd my schedule with other items of lesser value. Prioritizing helps us to keep what matters most at the center. Limiting the number of extra things that can get packed into a day also helps me to not have a hurried mindset.

READ 2 CORINTHIANS 1:12.

How does the culture impact your ability to live a life of simplicity?

_____

_____

Paul did not change how he conducted himself in the world. He was consistent. We don't have to let the world push us into its mold, either.

READ MATTHEW 6:31–33.

How does seeking God first help shape your priorities?

_____

_____

We don't have to be frantic like the world. We know our God is in control and if we seek Him first, everything falls into place. This does not mean that life will not have challenges, but it does mean we don't have to worry about what a sovereign God holds in His control.

READ 1 TIMOTHY 6:6–8.

What is of greater gain than striving?

_____

_____

Striving says we have added worry to our hurry. There is no need to strive when everything we have was given to us and ultimately it is God who we are accountable to. I can't imagine Jesus picking up His robe and running to do God's will. A slower pace leads to thriving rather than striving and works for me, too.

Day Five: Peaceful Diligence

"The plans of the diligent lead surely to abundance, but everyone who is hasty comes only to poverty."
Proverbs 21:5 ESV

Some people ask me how I do it all. This question bugs me. On top of this question is judgment that I am doing too much. We are to be diligent as we do what God has placed on our hearts, but that does not mean we have to be stressed about it. There are seasons in our lives where God accomplishes much and then there are seasons where we don't think we are fruitful, but the deeper work within us accomplishes so much more than any work we could ever do.

READ EPHESIANS 5:15–17.

What is the best use of our time?

_____

_____

Whenever I get into that familiar mode of wanting to work tirelessly to accomplish something that is on my heart, I remember I have nothing to offer if I have not first been fed. Diligence is not just in my work, it is in my devotion. My time is best used when I understand how God wants me to spend it.

READ MARK 1:35.

If Jesus needed to rise early to seek God, how much more do we? How do you fill your cup so you can pour into others?

_____

_____

Rise early or stay up late—wherever in your schedule it works, but I am a fan of rising early to seek Jesus. It shapes my mindset for the day. We won't rise early if we don't see time with God as a _need_. Seeking God before all else is not just a "good thing" to do. It is what shapes our relationship with God and our life. Without time spent with Jesus by reading God's Word and talking with Him, we are lost and can't help anybody.

READ 1 CORINTHIANS 15:58.

The non-hurried heart is still engaged in diligently serving God. What has God called you to do?

_____

_____

Diligence is part of what faithfulness to God's calling looks like, but diligence is not an excuse to be a workaholic. Giving ourselves to our work fully also means caring for those in our inner circle. Knowing the state of our heart as we press on toward our goals helps us do so with peaceful diligence.

READ PHILIPPIANS 3:14–17.

Paul strived and pressed on toward a goal. What was that goal?

_____

_____

We live in a culture that has selfish motivations rather than godly desires. Paul is such a good reminder of living intentionally with an inner motivation for God's glory and the sweet reward of simply being faithful to His calling. Don't forget the ultimate goal—your salvation and the salvation of others as they watch you live out your faith consistently.

Weekly Wrap-Up

Chapter Eight Reflection Questions

Which trigger did you identify with the most?

_____

_____

Which tip is your "go to strategy" when it comes to over-coming the hurried mindset?

_____

_____

How did Christ handle being hurried?

_____

_____

The Keys to Mindset Hacks

Write down the keys from chapter eight and any other insight that was significant to you.

Key Thought

_____

_____

Key Verse

_____

_____

Key Change

_____

_____

Counselor's Corner

Battling Hurriedness

Mindset Meditation

"Be still, and know that I am God! I will be honored by every nation. I will be honored throughout the world."
Psalm 46:10 NLT

When we exercise a muscle or practice a skill over and over again, we can train our bodies and minds to master a habit that doesn't come naturally. When I teach this to kids, I use the example of math facts. Ask any math teacher: repetition is the secret to success, far more than how smart a person is. If you want to truly master the act of being still and knowing He is God, you will need to practice stillness not only in your body but also your mind as you set aside time to focus on Him repeatedly.

As you breathe deeply and get in a comfortable position, breathe in stillness and breathe out any thoughts that come to mind, giving them to God. After you have nothing left to breathe out, repeat " be still" several times in your mind until you sense God's peace. Then repeat the word "know"

Make Up Your Mind (Study Guide)

until you sense His love. Finally, end your meditation time by repeating to yourself or aloud "You are God." Close this time without asking Him for anything or sharing anything with Him. Just receive.

Mindset Movement

Record on the lines below what it's like when you are still or how it felt to practice "spiritual breathing."

_____

_____

_____

_____

Questions for Connection

Share with your group what you learned from the Mindset Movements.

1. Share what it was like for you to practice stillness and "spiritual breathing" this week.
2. Which tasks that occur somewhat frequently in your life are you overestimating or underestimating the amount of time required to do them well?
3. When is the best daily and weekly time for you to schedule down time?
4. What techniques from this Counselor's Corner will you use to take breaks from your thoughts?

Additional Resources

Redeeming Your Time: 7 Biblical Principles for Being Purposeful, Present, and Wildly Productive by Jordan Raynor

Take Back Your Time: Identify Your Priorities, Decrease Stress, and Increase Productivity by Morgan Tyree

The Ruthless Elimination of Hurry: How to Stay Emotionally Healthy and Spiritually Alive in the Chaos of the Modern World by John Mark Comer and John Ortberg

Notes or Questions from Chapter Reading

_____

_____

_____

_____

_____

_____

_____

_____

_____

_____

_____

_____

_____

_____

_____

_____

WEEK NINE

"Turn to me and be gracious to me, for I am lonely and afflicted."

Psalm 25:16 ESV

Chapter 9

The Lonely Mindset: Battling Grief and Isolation

"God places the lonely in families; he sets the prisoners free and gives them joy. But he makes the rebellious live in a sun-scorched land."
Psalm 68:6 NLT

I remember sitting alone for most of my lunches when I was in college. I was an introvert who marveled at people who were so personable and had so much confidence. Some would say that was just how I was wired, but life had built me that way. Multiple divorces by my parents and more moves than my two hands could count left me feeling unstable and isolated. Bullying coupled with abuse left me feeling even more isolated and lonely. Did anyone care? Did anyone see me? Looking at other peoples' situations only increased my pain.

But feelings of loneliness do not mean we are not wanted. It might be that loneliness pushes us to seek out companionship we would not have found had we not first encountered loneliness.

As I grew older, got married, and had children, loneliness did not seem a likely companion. But loneliness is not a discriminator of people, and it is not confined to one stage of life. It can hit you out of nowhere and make you feel so small. Knowing how to battle through our grief and isolation will help us rest in the companionship an identity in Christ offers.

Day One: The Lonely Soul

"O Lord, all my longing is before you; my sighing is not hidden from you."
Psalm 38:9 ESV

Somewhere in our souls is a need to be seen. But our need does not stop there. We want to know we have significance. I wish I could tell 12-year-old and 17-year-old Denise that she would never have more significance than she already had in Jesus' eyes. Christ demonstrated our worth by dying for us but sometimes we want flesh and blood to give us our worth. This sets us up for failure, for no one could consistently feed the lonely monster's constant need for affirmation.

READ GENESIS 16:1–4.

Manipulated and mistreated, Hagar had reason to not be a fan of Sarah. Have you endured mistreatment that is hard to let go of?

_____

_____

READ GENESIS 16:5–6.

Things went from bad to worse. Sarah caused the mess and blamed Abram for it—dysfunction at its finest. Hagar could not defend herself. Pregnant and unwanted, loneliness was at an all-time high. Who did Sarai ask to judge the situation?

_____

_____

We all have likely had a moment where we were put at the mercy of the hands of an enemy. Not fun. Not fair. At first we are thrilled that God noticed Hagar. We identify with her on some level, don't we? But then we also hope for her to be rescued. Was she?

READ GENESIS 16:7–9.

Does this feel fair to you?

_____

_____

God's command to Hagar did not mean that He did not see her plight or that He did not care. He was taking care of her, even if the situation was less than ideal. But the difference was now Hagar knew she was not alone. God's presence was with her, and He made a promise to her about her future.

READ GENESIS 16:11–13.

Why did God seeing Hagar mean so much when He left her in the same situation?

_____

_____

Sometimes we just want to be removed from our loneliness. We want God's deliverance. But sometimes God meets us in our suffering and gives us grace we did not expect. God sent Hagar back to the lonely place she came from. What can we learn from this? Loneliness is not a place. It is a state of the mind. God wants to meet us in that place just like He met Hagar.

READ PSALM 9:9–10.

Can you trust God in your loneliness? He is with us and can heal our loneliness. Write a prayer and make God your refuge. He surrounds you and He is Your comfort.

_____

_____

Being seen by God was enough for Hagar. It can be enough for us, too, if we will prize the presence of God more than the presence of man. God knows we need fellowship but He also wants to make us whole so we can have healthy fellowship with others as we depend on God and not people for our worth.

Make Up Your Mind (Study Guide)

Day Two: The Wounded Soul

*"For my father and my mother have forsaken
me, but the Lord will take me in."*
Psalm 27:10 ESV

Wounds in this world leave us broken. So much so, that we begin to view life through a broken lens. If we are not careful, our brokenness leads to isolation as we think no one will understand us. The wounds of our soul can deepen when we doubt that God sees us in our pain. We don't have to be loyal to our pain. Knowing God sees us reminds us that He will take care of us. He bore our wounds for us and He is our Healer.

READ PSALM 147:3.

Have you felt like your wounds are beyond healing? Why or why not?

_____

_____

READ PSALM 34:17–20.

How many troubles did God deliver the righteous from?

_____

_____

We struggle to believe our problems matter to God. In part our faith might be wounded that God allowed our pain in the first place. And when He does not remove our pain, we feel even more wounded. But perhaps not removing the thorn in our flesh reminds us that with or without sorrow, God is enough.

READ 2 CORINTHIANS 12:7–10.

Have you had suffering in your life that God has not removed? How did it make you feel?

_____

_____

When my oldest daughter was diagnosed with Celiac Disease, I was so grateful . . . and overwhelmed. I remember crying out and asking God if things would ever be easy again. "No" was the response in my spirit. "My grace is sufficient for you." I learned in that moment not to crave the absence of sorrow, but to look to God *in* my sorrows.

Day Three: The Fruit of Isolation

"Whoever isolates himself seeks his own desire;
he breaks out against all sound judgment."
Proverbs 18:1 ESV

I remember when I was the last one to be picked on teams when I was growing up. Only I wasn't even picked then. The last person picking *had* to pick me. Being on the team did not make me feel a part of the team at all. I was still isolated, even though I was surrounded by many. In fact, the entire team made up some gossip, so they had an excuse to beat me up. Good times. Being isolated makes us vulnerable to attack from the enemy, whether by choice or not. But the lonely have an advocate who was also accustomed to loneliness.

READ 1 SAMUEL 12:22.

How does it make you feel to know you are a part of God's team?

_____

_____

You belong. God was pleased to invite you onto His team and you did not do a thing to earn your place. You cannot lose that position because His grace is what earned your spot.

READ ROMANS 8:35–39.

Sometimes we feel lonely because we are isolated from others. How does the reality that nothing can separate you from God speak to your loneliness?

_____

_____

READ 1 JOHN 4:13.

How do we access God's presence when we feel nothing but absence in this life?

_____

_____

The Holy Spirit is the evidence of God's presence. The fruit of isolation is bad fruit, friends. Proverbs 18:1 reminds us that isolating ourselves causes us to lose sound judgment. Having other people we are accountable to helps us bounce ideas off them to check ourselves. No man is an island, or at least he should not be.

Day Four: The Consolation of Company

"Not neglecting to meet together, as is the habit of some, but encouraging one another, and all the more as you see the Day drawing near."
Hebrews 10:25 ESV

Where two or more are gathered you have conflict. And drama. And issues. But God set it up so His people would be in community with one another. Company has a way of refining us if we show up and do life together. The early church were people of community. They were not an individualistic culture. Today it is easy to become separated with the advent of social media, but we must press in toward community for this is where we are able to encourage one another to stay on mission in Christ.

READ GENESIS 2:18.

God's design is that we remain in fellowship with other believers. Why do you think God does not want us to be alone?

_____

_____

Living out in the boonies, I have observed what can happen when birds leave home too soon. The enemy can easily pick off those who separate from the flock. It is the same with us. Don't avoid accountability because you want to be independent. That independence might cost you greatly.

READ 1 CORINTHIANS 12:14.

Having many members in the body of Christ means we don't have to be alone. But we might have to search for a good group to be involved with. Whenever my children have moved somewhere new, I always challenged them to position themselves for godly fellowship. Church, small groups, Bible studies. This made the biggest difference to them! Do you have accountability in your life through people you allow to speak into your life?

_____

_____

Sometimes lonely people compromise and hang out with people who pull them far away from God's purposes.

READ 1 CORINTHIANS 15:33.

Do you find it hard to find godly friends? Are you careful in the company you keep?

_____

_____

Who can you reach out to today? Don't let shame (embarrassment) keep you from praying and thinking about someone God might have you reach out to. Oftentimes we avoid company because we don't want to put forth the effort or face rejection. Write down a name of 1 or 2 people and reach out to them. Get coffee or just call and encourage them. Admitting we need fellowship is not a weakness—it is walking in God's plan.

Day Five: The Secret of Solitude

"But when you pray, go into your room and shut the door and pray to your Father who is in secret. And your Father who sees in secret will reward you."
Matthew 6:6 ESV

If we are always surrounded by people, we cannot be still. I know, I know, I just told you that you need to seek out company. Yes, you do. But balance is important. I am entering the empty nest season in my life and have had a lingering sadness that my children are not all around me. We communicate regularly, but things had to change. It would be unhealthy if they did not. Yet there is also a beauty in this season. I love getting up early or staying up late just to meet with God alone. This time of solitude never makes me feel alone.

READ MATTHEW 6:6.

How do you make time for solitude?

_____

_____

READ MARK 6:31.

Can you feel the hecticness of their environment? They could not even eat. There is a phrase "if you don't come apart, you will come apart". Do you see your need for solitude?

_____

_____

If Jesus needed solitude, how much more do we? And it is interesting that Jesus did not just model it, but he encouraged His disciples to also make time for solitude.

READ MATTHEW 14:23.

Solitude is different from loneliness or isolation. It is an opportunity to feed our weary souls and suddenly we discover we are not lonely anymore. When my children were little, it seemed impossible to have my devotional time with Jesus. I would rise earlier only to find a toddler with a binky (pacifier) waiting for me. So I learned to have my time with Jesus right in front of them all. We might have to be creative with how we fit this time in, but don't miss it! How are you able to have times of solitude in your life?

_____

_____

READ MARK 1:35.

Jesus made a habit with his times of solitude, and He stuck with it. The secret of solitude is that we don't feel alone when we rest in His perfect presence. Solitude has a way of awakening us to things we did not see before. We cannot hide behind distractions. It is just us and our Maker. Solitude brings us clarity and peace. It might feel stressful to carve out the time, but you will be so glad you did. As we sit in stillness before God, we are seen, and we see ourselves in the light of His presence. Take a couple minutes right now and let yourself think without distraction. Interact with God's Word. Pray. Just be. Write down what He brings to your mind during this time.

_____

_____

_____

_____

Weekly Wrap-Up

Chapter Nine Reflection Questions

Which trigger did you identify with the most?

_____

_____

Which tip is your "go to strategy" when it comes to over-coming the lonely mindset?

_____

_____

How did Christ handle loneliness?

_____

_____

The Keys to Mindset Hacks

Write down the keys from chapter nine and any other insight that was significant to you.

Key Thought

_____

_____

Key Verse

_____

_____

Key Change

_____

_____

Counselor's Corner

Battling Loneliness

Mindset Meditation

*"Turn to me and be gracious to me, for I
am lonely and afflicted."*
Psalm 25:16 NIV

"Grandma, I don't want to leave," I said as we sat in her assisted living room.

"I don't want you to be alone."

My grandmother smiled at me and shared these words I'll never forget: "Michelle, I cannot remember a single time in my life when I felt alone because I've always known God is with me."

Not all of us are blessed with experiencing God like my grandmother. During your meditation time, cry out to God and see Him comforting you in a way the brings you peace and makes you feel loved. A comforting image for me is to envision myself under the shadow of His wings, completely protected, covered, and securely held (Psalm 61:4). Rest in His comfort as long as you can.

Describe how you experience the comfort of God.

_____

_____

_____

_____

Mindset Movement

What was it like to be intentional about making plans with someone? Reflect upon the last time you spent quality time with a friend.

_____

_____

_____

_____

Questions for Connection

1. Share about how you experienced the comfort of God during your Mindset Meditation time.
2. Share about one person you reached out to and how it went. Let the group celebrate with you if it went well and encourage you to keep trying if it wasn't a good match for you. Friendships are a lot like dating. They often start out awkward and take time to reach a comfortable level. You will also spend time with

some people and know after one encounter you probably aren't a good match for a long-time friendship.
3. Which of the three obstacles to creating community is
the most challenging for you, and why?
4. Which one is harder for you—listening or talking?
What next step do you need to take so you can connect well with others?
5. Share a few names of some friends or family you can
text or call next time you feel lonely.

Additional Resources

Safe People: How to Find Relationships that are Good for You and Avoid Those That Aren't by Henry Cloud and John Townsend

Uninvited: Living Loved When You Feel Less Than, Left Out, and Lonely by Lysa TerKeurst

The Seven Deadly Friendships: How to Heal When Painful Relationships Eat Away at Your Joy by Mary Demuth

Find Your People: Building Deep Community in a Lonely World by Jennie Allen

Notes or Questions from Chapter Reading

_____

_____

_____

_____

_____

_____

_____

_____

_____

_____

_____

_____

_____

_____

_____

_____

WEEK TEN

"The Lord is my portion,' says my soul, 'therefore I will hope in him."

Lamentations 3:24 ESV

Chapter 10

The Scarcity Mindset— Battling Covetousness and Lust

"My flesh and my heart may fail, but God is the strength of my heart and my portion forever."
Psalm 73:26 ESV

The irony in the scarcity mentality is that those who struggle with it fear not having enough, though they likely have plenty. We can struggle for a portion or the lot in this life we think we deserve but miss the portion God has given us. No other portion will satisfy. We might not even recognize our discontent with what we have until comparison exacerbates our discontent attitude and brings the scarcity mindset to the forefront.

The three core sins of man—lust of the flesh, lust of the eyes, and boastful pride of life—are seen in the scarcity mindset. The lust of the eyes is wanting what is not our portion (jealousy, coveting). The lust of the flesh is craving according to the flesh to excess (gluttony, adultery, idolatry). And the pride of life is absorption in self (self-promotion, greed). This leads us to feel like we never have enough as we compare to others and look at what we think is inadequate in ourselves. But when we make God our portion rather than anything in this world, we cease trying to make an idol out of God's provision and look to our Provider, instead.

Day One: How Much is Enough?

"All things are wearisome, more than one can say. The eye never has enough of seeing, nor the ear its fill of hearing."
Ecclesiastes 1:8 NIV

Pulling up in the driveway hours before I expected my husband, I knew there was probably some difficult news I was about to hear. Another layoff. Another opportunity to exercise faith and walk with God through lean times. We had been in this position before. Only this time in my spirit I knew it was going to be at least 8 months. But God also provided abundant faith to walk through a season of lack. Miracles happened. God provided out of nothing something that I will never forget. I learned that little is much in the hands of God. The question was no longer would we have enough, as God always provides what we need.

READ ECCLESIASTES 5:10.

Taxes and the cost of living can make us all feel like we will not have enough, but what is the main word in this Scripture that points to one reason why we might not have enough?

_____

_____

Loving wealth is an indication of idolatry. If we love material belongings, they cannot satisfy spiritual longings and will never be enough.

READ PROVERBS 25:16.

Our culture thinks it funny to overindulge. Ads encourage us to splurge . . . 'cause we deserve it. Such overindulgence is a prescription for lots of health problems. What does this Scripture say will happen if we overindulge?

_____

_____

I shared about my struggle to be satisfied with less in the book, *Make Up Your Mind*. As we get older, our bodies do not require as many calories. I have learned that craving more than I need is not blessing me or my body. It is not a treat to eat more than what is enough for my temple, which houses God. When I don't make an idol out of my portion but use my portion to fuel me for God's service, it is a witness to the world of self-control.

READ MATTHEW 14:16–18.

You can see the gears turning in the disciples' minds. How could so little feed so many? But they were operating on what they had, not on what God could do with what they had. Have you ever had a time when you did not have enough in your view, but God multiplied what you had?

_____

_____

READ MATTHEW 14:19–21.

What did Jesus do with what He was given?

_____

_____

Sometimes we need to express gratitude for the portion we have rather than assessing that it is not enough. My children remember feeling scared when we were in that lengthy season without. But then they also remember our faith and God's goodness and how God made something out of seemingly nothing. Such times end up being a holy place of interaction with God showing up to meet our need every time. Perhaps if we always had enough we would not understand what it is to be truly satisfied.

Day Two: How Much is Too Much?

*"But when they measured it with an omer,
whoever gathered much had nothing left over,
and whoever gathered little had no lack. Each of
them gathered as much as he could eat."*
Exodus 16:18. ESV

How much is enough? Out of fear, we can pile up extra to make sure we will never be lacking. During Y2K (so dubbed because it referred to the year 2000), many people stocked up on excessive food to make sure they would not be without. I admit I was one of them. In recent years, during the pandemic of 2020, people bought so much toilet paper there was a shortage. It is interesting that this was the prime item at such a time, but I digress. In our provision, it is easy to forget that God doesn't want us to build bigger barns for security. He is our security and Jehovah Jireh, our Provider. Any blessing He pours out on us is so we can pour it out on others for the glory of God.

READ PHILIPPIANS 4:19.

Knowing that God supplies our every need should be comforting but sometimes we might feel like He won't provide our wants, too, if we are honest. Share how God has provided for your needs.

_____

_____

God literally fed His people with food from Heaven. I don't know what that Manna must have tasted like – the Bible describes it as bread (Exodus 16:15), or a sweet wafer with honey (Exodus 16:31). Yum. Being the carb lover I am, I am sure I would have loved it! However, there are lessons to learn from how the Israelites treated God's provision.

READ EXODUS 16:16–18.

It is interesting that the amount varied according to what the person thought they needed. How much did they all gather?

_____

_____

READ EXODUS 16:19.

Why do you think God did not want them to save some for the next day?

_____

_____

Leftovers are the bomb at our house. They give me a break from cooking the next day. But some of my children don't like leftovers. They want to eat something new. God was not disallowing leftovers. God was teaching the Israelites that He was trustworthy. He wanted His people to rely on Him to provide for them each day. He did not want them to gather too much, but just enough. That is hard for us, too, isn't it? But our security should not come from our ability to save ourselves, but

God's. We should still be diligent and wise with what God provides, but not look to our ability as much as God's.

READ EXODUS 16:20.

Why did the Israelites not listen?

_____

_____

The Israelites complained about what God provided (Exodus 16:2–3), how much God provided, and how God provided. The Israelites accused God of sinister motivations—wanting to kill them—when the provision seemed lean in their eyes. (Exodus 16:3, Exodus 17:3). At the root of the scarcity mindset is a problem in our relationship with God. God's provision is an opportunity to walk in relationship with Him, trusting Him and being grateful for whatever portion He provides. Our talents, our finances, and our relationships are ours, not somebody else's. Will we be faithful with what He has provided?

Day Three: Taming Our Temptations

"But each person is tempted when he is lured and enticed by his own desire."
James 1:14 ESV

We don't have to give into the scarcity mindset. Having more will not heal a hungry soul. We tame our temptations when we stop looking for satisfaction from creation and look to our Creator instead. Walking in the Spirit helps us rise above the flesh. As we begin to see when we are tempted to have a scarcity mindset, we can meet that temptation with an answer from God's Word, just like Jesus did (Matthew 4:1–11). God's Word is our food and our portion. Nothing in this world will satisfy.

READ 1 JOHN 2:16.

It is difficult to grow up in a world and not adopt its desires and fads. What temptation do you have toward a scarcity mindset?

_____

_____

Self-control is not just for some people. The fruit of the Spirit was given to all who believe in Jesus and that includes self-control. But it will not be easy.

READ 1 CORINTHIANS 10:13.

What way out has God provided for you in this temptation you listed above?

_____

_____

READ JAMES 1:14.

What causes your struggle with the scarcity mindset?

_____

_____

We will not have victory until we admit our need. We need to own the fact that we struggle. But we don't have to stay there. Repentance brings sweet relief. Admit your struggle and ask Jesus to help. He always will.

READ HEBREWS 2:18.

Do you believe Jesus can help you when you are tempted with a scarcity mindset?

_____

_____

Tomorrow we will look at how to turn our scarcity mindset to a mindset of abundance.

Day Four: Learning to Have an Abundance Mindset

"Give thanks in all circumstances; for this is the will of God in Christ Jesus for you."
1 Thessalonians 5:18 ESV

Gratitude is the catalyst that takes one from a scarcity mindset to an abundance mindset. But gratitude does not flow from someone who does not recognize how blessed they are. We don't have to "feel" gratitude to be grateful. It might start out as crying out to God and asking Him to help you. Then reading His Word out loud can remind us of the blessings we have. We must instruct our heart, rather than our heart instructing our mindset. Hard circumstances try to crush gratitude, but true gratitude happens right in the middle of hard places as we discover that we would not have gratitude had we not first experienced suffering.

READ PSALM 118:22–24.

Is this Scripture an invitation to rejoice only in what we dub as good days? Why can we rejoice in every day, even the hard ones?

_____

_____

Our good days were purchased with Christ's worst days as He faced rejection to give us His acceptance. The salvation Christ offers us helps us to rise above the hardest days. Our eternity is secured. Temporary hardship pales in light of eternity.

READ PSALM 136:1.

How does God's goodness put life's "badness" into perspective?

_____

_____

READ HEBREWS 12:28–29.

What are we to be grateful for?

_____

_____

We are heirs of a Kingdom that cannot be shaken. When we take our eyes off what we think is our lack and fix it on the incredible riches we have in Christ, we foster an abundance mindset. We have more than we deserve.

Day Five: The Secret of Contentment

> "Now there is great gain in godliness with contentment, for we brought nothing into the world, and we cannot take anything out of the world. But if we have food and clothing, with these we will be content."
> 1 Timothy 6:6–8 ESV

It can be overwhelming to focus on our perceived lack. But when we take the focus off ourselves and help others, suddenly we are content with what we have. Godliness with contentment helps us understand this life isn't just about us and getting our needs met. Godliness helps us keep an eternal, Heavenly perspective rather than a worldly one. The scarcity mindset dissolves when we learn to be content with what God has given.

READ HEBREWS 13:5.

Why should we be content?

_____

_____

God with us is enough. We have all we need with Him. Nothing in this world can make such a guarantee.

READ LUKE 12:15.

What should life consist of?

_____

_____

It is not the abundance of possessions that gives us life, but the abundance of God's presence.

READ LUKE 12:22–23.

What is at the root of our desire to have more?

_____

_____

Anxiety pushes us to strive for more and worry about what we have. But God helps us find contentment that is far greater than the temporal contentment of provision in the world.

READ LUKE 12:29–31.

How do we heal a discontented heart that is always thinking about our provision?

_____

_____

Seeking God helps us to stop seeking the world to comfort our feelings of scarcity. And the irony is that holding on tightly to what we own will not bring us the abundance mentality as much as giving to others will. During another lean season in my life, God blessed our garden more than any year before, and we were able to bless others. Oh, the overwhelming joy that was in our hearts probably would not have been there had we not experienced lack first.

READ LUKE 12:32–34.

What else is at the root of the scarcity mindset?

_____

_____

Fear keeps us bound in the scarcity mindset, but trusting God frees us to no longer be paralyzed by fear, but to become His vessels to help provide for others.

Weekly Wrap-Up

Chapter Ten Reflection Questions

Which trigger did you identify with the most?

_____

_____

Which tip is your "go to strategy" when it comes to over-coming the scarcity mindset?

_____

_____

How did Christ handle scarcity?

_____

_____

The Keys to Mindset Hacks

Write down the keys from chapter ten and any other insight that was a significant to you!

Key Thought

_____

_____

Key Verse

_____

_____

Key Change

_____

_____

Counselor's Corner

Battling Scarcity and Jealousy

Mindset Meditation

> *"So we fix our eyes not on what is seen,*
> *but on what is unseen, since what is seen is*
> *temporary, but what is unseen is eternal."*
> 2 Corinthians 4:18 NIV

I believe God created me to appreciate beauty. When we see something that we find desirable, the neurotransmitter dopamine releases in our brain and creates an instant pathway of pleasure throughout our nervous system. While delighting in the seen can bring me joy, obsessing on an earthly object has never satisfied my soul. Ask any gamer or addict, dopamine fades more quickly than they desire, and it takes more and more of whatever they crave to create that surge that once satisfied completely.

Let's start our meditation by getting in a comfortable position in a place where you are not likely to be interrupted. Next, we are going to work on calming your amygdala (the part of your brain that experiences hyperarousal often described as a fight, in a fight, flight, or freeze mode) by taking some deep breaths, this time alternating in through one nostril and out through the other. Alternating breathing in and out of each nostril calms many people's nervous systems more than just deep breathing alone.

Finally, spend some time intentionally directing your thoughts toward the unseen. You can meditate on the words in Philippians 4:8 or Galatians 5:22-23, which are unseen virtues that build us up.

Record on the lines below what aspects of the unseen you focused on during your time of meditation.

_____

_____

_____

_____

Mindset Movement

Look up John 10:10 and write it on the lines below. Then write out a phrase aligned with Scripture or a Bible verse that will remind you of the abundant life you've been promised.

_____

_____

_____

_____

Questions for Connection

Share with your group what you learned from the Mindset Movements.

1. Share some words that reminded you of the unseen upon which you meditated.

2. If you completed Mindset Movement #2 for this chapter in the book and practiced mindfulness around someone this week, share what it was like to be fully present and engaged instead of distracted and overwhelmed.

3. Describe some purchases that gave you pleasure (love that dopamine) in the moment but in time no longer brought you the same level of joy. Also, feel free to share about something seen that still brings you joy. See if you can discern what, if anything, is different about that purchase.

4. What three non-material things are you thankful for today?

5. What has God done with the "loaves and fishes" you offered Him in the past? What might He do with your offerings now? If you are in a season where you are desperate for God to work when you are not working, share about those life demands or callings.

Additional Resources

Didn't See It Coming: Overcoming the Seven Greatest Challenges That No One Expects and Everyone Experiences by Carey Nieuwhof

Undistracted: Capture Your Purpose. Rediscover Your Joy by Bob Goff

Make Up Your Mind (Study Guide)

Notes or Questions from Chapter Reading

WEEK ELEVEN

"Blessed be the God and Father of our Lord Jesus Christ, the Father of mercies and God of all comfort, who comforts us in all our affliction, so that we may be able to comfort those who are in any affliction, with the comfort with which we ourselves are comforted by God."

2 Corinthians 1:3-4 ESV

Chapter 11

The Victim Mindset— Battling Insecurity and Rejection

"But you, God, see the trouble of the afflicted;
you consider their grief and take it in hand. The
victims commit themselves to you; you are the
helper of the fatherless."
Psalm 10:14 NIV

Like the lonely mindset that feels unseen, the victim mindset is provoked by this same sense of no one commiserating or having compassion on our plight. I don't think we are ever ready for affliction. It catches us by surprise, but perhaps it shouldn't. A broken world cannot deliver on the hopes we have. It can only serve to ultimately crush them. And broken people can never give the comfort or significance God does.

I spent a good portion of my life feeling rejected. There was some truth to the rejection I felt. I was not popular. I won the "ugly" award in Girl Scouts at a sleepover when my jammies were, well, not cute. They gave me a comb for a prize. Then there was the time when I had rocks thrown at me and was called an unkind name for the color of my skin. Worthless in their eyes. Or the time when someone told me they could no longer take me to the school dance because I was not popular. The stories could go on and on. The acceptance I longed for from those who should have freely given it in my inner sphere just caused the victim mindset to blossom even more within the walls of my mind. The wounds of childhood shape us, but then, we should never have been looking to the creation for acceptance.

When I was saved in 1988, God, my Abba Father, showed me the acceptance I had not seen all along. The poor self-worth and insecurity that raged within were calmed in His sweet presence. But habits formed from victimhood take a while to heal. God's Word is able to do that work. Are you ready?

Day One: Dealing with Unfairness

*"Consider him who endured such opposition
from sinners, So that you will not
grow weary and lose heart."*
Hebrews 12:3 ESV

There is something ironic about our sense of injustice over life being unfair. We did not get what we deserve from a Holy God—judgment for our sin. The sooner we accept life's unfairness, the sooner we are able to stay focused on God's purposes in the pain. Unfairness is flipped on its head in the Kingdom of God. We will have to endure hardship in this life, but God is with us.

READ 2 CORINTHIANS 4:7–12.

The harshness of life can leave us jaded if we do not view it through a biblical lens. What does this Scripture say about Paul's perspective in the face of unfairness?

_____

_____

Our mindset does not have to give in to our circumstances. The Holy Spirit empowers those who are in Christ to walk in victory.

READ PHILIPPIANS 4:6–7.

What will guard your heart and mind when you encounter unfair situations? What is our part?

_____

_____

READ ROMANS 8:28.

What does God promise to do with all the things we go through in this life?

_____

_____

What a Redeemer we have! Tomorrow we will explore God's acceptance of us and how His acceptance heals man's rejection and makes us victors in Christ.

Day Two: Finding Acceptance

"Show me the wonders of your great love, you who save by your right hand those who take refuge in you from their foes."
Psalm 17:7 ESV

Oh, how much time I have wasted worshiping at the altar of acceptance. Acceptance that I already had but my mind still wanted man's praise. When it seems the world is against us, it is overwhelming, and we can let rejection label or define us as we are engulfed in shame. But there is a refuge to be found by those willing to lay down the world's embrace. We find our acceptance by letting go of man's approval.

READ ROMANS 5:8.

How does God's acceptance speak to your rejection from others?

_____

_____

When we were at our worst, God set His love on us. If God, the One Who rules the world, has accepted us, why do we let man's acceptance bother us so much? We have the victory!

_____

_____

READ ROMANS 2:11.

God is fair when man is not. Why is this significant?

_____

_____

We can waste a lot of time worrying about things not being fair, but knowing that the perfect Judge of the universe does not show favoritism yet forgives all our sins is the highest favor of all.

READ 1 SAMUEL 16:7.

What does God look at and what hope does this give you when man does not accept you?

_____

_____

God sees us and knows us fully. While this can be a scary thing to consider in the presence of a holy God, God looks at our hearts and does not reject those who trust in Him. Tomorrow we will look at the role that suffering plays in our victim status and how perspective is everything.

232

Day Three: Perspective in Suffering

"Blessed is the one who perseveres under trial
because, having stood the test, that person
will receive the crown of life that the Lord has
promised to those who love him."
James 1:12 ESV

James (James 1:2–4), Paul (Romans 5:3–5), and Peter (1 Peter 4:13) all have in common their encouragement to count suffering as joy. Oh joy. We want a pity party, don't we? But pity parties cannot help us in our suffering—they just keep us in a prison of suffering, bound by a victim mindset. The hospital has been my training ground for joy. In the greatest suffering of my life, God shifted my gaze off my pain and onto His mission for me in that space. Oh, how precious those moments of transformation are to me now. Perspective in suffering helps us persevere. Trials are temporary, but how we walk them out impacts those around us possibly for eternity.

READ 2 CORINTHIANS 12:10.

Who is our suffering for?

_____

_____

The phrase, "for my sake" is used 40+ times in Scripture, always alluding to God (20 times in the OT) or Christ (20 times in the NT). This gives meaning to our suffering. No suffering is in vain. And when we walk through our suffering for God's glory, we discover a strength that enables us to walk through that suffering.

READ ROMANS 5:3–5.

What is the fruit of suffering?

_____

_____

READ 1 PETER 5:10

Who is our comforter in suffering?

_____

_____

If we did not walk through suffering, we would not experience the comfort and peace that God gives us in that place of suffering. Perspective is born there. This life is not about being comfortable. It is about being faithful at all times, for the glory of God.

READ ROMANS 8:18.

Does the future hope that God has for you encourage you in your suffering?

_____

_____

I love how John Piper describes the superior pleasure of what God has in store for His people. It makes the temporary problems of the here and now so small. God can give us this perspective, but we will have to trust Him. Pain gets our attention and can hold us hostage. But we do not have to stay there. God came to endure suffering to win our souls. His grace is sufficient for us to walk through our suffering as well.

Day Four: Letting God Fight for You

> *"For the weapons of our warfare are not of the flesh but have divine power to destroy strongholds."*
> 2 Corinthians 10:4 ESV

Fight or flight. These are the two choices we are given when we face battles. But there is another shocking option we can choose. Be still. In middle school, threats and fights were common. Fridays were when knife fights happened, and this girl skipped school if she could. I was called "chicken" and heartily agreed. I did not want to fight anyone. The weapons people fight with can be fearsome, but they cannot compare with God's. God defended and protected me more than I realized in that season of my life. Now as a believer, I know where my help comes from. Still, I can be tempted to give in to fear if I try to fight my battles on my own.

READ JOSHUA 10:25.

Hidden in God's command is a truth about our mindsets. What is it?

_____

_____

The phrase, "do not be afraid or discouraged" is repeated like a mantra in the book of Joshua. This command was an encouragement and a reminder that we have a choice. We don't have to give into fear or discouragement. And when we fight battles in the mind or in our lives, our God fights for us. Throughout Scripture we see another phrase, "the LORD your God fights for you." Will you let Him?

READ EXODUS 14:14.

What is our role in the battle of our mind?

_____

_____

READ 2 CHRONICLES 20:17.

What other tactics should we employ in battles we face?

_____

_____

READ DEUTERONOMY 3:22.

The reality of God's defense should cause us to do what?

_____

_____

READ ISAIAH 43:2.

We are not promised a battle-free life, but we are promised God's presence. How does the reality of God with us help you in times of battle?

_____

_____

READ EPHESIANS 6:10.

What are we to be strong in?

_____

_____

READ PHILIPPIANS 4:13.

How are you strengthened through Christ?

_____

_____

Day Five: From Victim to Victor

"But thanks be to God, who gives us the
victory through our Lord Jesus Christ."
1 Corinthians 15:57 ESV

Jesus' question to the lame man as recorded in John 5:6 seems like an obvious one. "Do you want to get well?" But sometimes we don't have faith to believe that we will. Or maybe we have grown accustomed to our victim status and have worn that status like an identity and just don't have any fight left. God is asking us the same question today when we feel like a victim. "Do you want to get well?" Victimhood is an illness, too. It keeps us from walking in victory.

READ 1 PETER 2:19–21.

What does bearing our victimhood with Christ in mind earn us?

_____

_____

We earn a reward for suffering endured for the sake of Christ in this life. Keeping this reality in mind helps to put our struggles in the right place.

READ 1 PETER 4:19.

Who should we trust in our suffering?

_____

_____

The world likes to blame God in their suffering, but when we entrust ourselves to God in our suffering, we defeat the victim mindset and become a victor. Nick Vujicic, a man born without arms or legs is such an example of not choosing the victim status. He has used his hardship as a platform to preach the Gospel. How about us? The rain falls on everyone. How we bear that rain might be the very thing that draws someone to know Jesus.

READ ROMANS 12:21.

What are we supposed to do when evil befalls us?

_____

_____

Wow, what sweet victory it is when we don't allow anything in this life to make us a victim. In Christ, we understand that no suffering is ever wasted in the hands of God. In Christ, we do not need to compare our suffering to someone else's suffering. In Christ, we understand that our suffering in the Lord earns us rewards in Heaven. Wear your suffering well, friend. God is using it to shape you into His image and to help others see Him in you.

Weekly Wrap-Up

Chapter Eleven Reflection Questions

Which trigger did you identify with the most?

_____

_____

Which tip is your "go to strategy" when it comes to over-coming the victim mindset?

_____

_____

How did Christ handle victimhood?

_____

_____

The Keys to Mindset Hacks

Write down the keys from chapter eleven and any other insight that was significant to you.

Key Thought

_____

_____

Key Verse

_____

_____

Key Change

_____

_____

Counselor's Corner

Battling the Victim Mindset

Mindset Meditation

"But thanks be to God! He gives us the victory through our Lord Jesus Christ."
1 Corinthians 15:57 NIV

Meditation doesn't always have to occur in a passive, relaxed position. For this Mindset Meditation, I'd like you to choose an active pose that represents "victory" to you. Amy Cuddy in her Ted Talk* on body language teaches how many people report positive life results from holding power poses for two minutes. *(www.youtube.com/watch?v=Ks-_Mh1QhMc)

A few options you might consider would be holding your hands up high, taking a "wonder woman" pose with your hands on your hips and your legs out a little wider than hip distance, or for many Christians who believe surrender to God is our most powerful position, it might be kneeling. While you are in your victory position, thank God either silently or aloud claiming your victory in Jesus.

List on the lines below some areas of your life in which you are currently trusting God to bring you victory. You may also want to reinforce how your power pose impacted your emotional well-being. If you found it positive, try doing this meditation daily for two minutes and notice any changes in your confidence level. Don't forget your God focus as self-help alone doesn't provide the same power as He provides.

_____

_____

_____

_____

Mindset Movement

Scripture teaches when we experience pain at the hands of another on this earth, they are not our enemy, but Satan is (Ephesians 6:12). The next time you are in conflict with someone, visualize in your mind that you and the person you disagree with are wearing sticky notes on your foreheads that say "I am not your enemy" to remind you that your battle isn't earthly but spiritual.

Questions for Connection

Share with your group what you learned from the Mindset Movements.

1. If you did the Mindset Movement exercise for this chapter, share with the group how it went.
2. Have you or someone you know ever been part of a "drama triangle"? What did you learn from that experience?
3. What can you do differently to avoid having a victim mindset in the future?
4. Who do you need to admit you cannot change, and what changes can you make within yourself so that you can better manage a difficult relationship in your life?

Additional Resources

Boundaries for Your Soul: How to Turn Your Overwhelming Thoughts and Feelings into Your Greatest Allies by Alison Cook, Ph.D., and Kimberly Miller, M.Th. L.M.F.T.

Changes That Heal: Four Practical Steps to a Happier, Healthier You by Henry Cloud

Notes or Questions from Chapter Reading

_____

_____

_____

_____

_____

_____

_____

_____

_____

_____

_____

_____

_____

_____

_____

WEEK TWELVE

"Repent [change your inner self—your old way of thinking, regret past sins, live your life in a way that proves repentance; seek God's purpose for your life], for the kingdom of heaven is at hand."

Matthew 3:2 AMP

Chapter 12

🗝 *The Mind of Christ*

"For, 'Who has known the mind of the Lord so as to instruct him?' But we have the mind of Christ."
1 Corinthians 2:16 NIV

As I began my research into the mind of Christ, I was searching for something I did not understand. I thought that perhaps my whole Christian walk I was missing something and perhaps many others were, too. The defeated lives around me and my own struggles made me think there was more than what many were experiencing. In truth, yes, there were many missing something in their walk with God. But it wasn't because they had not received something from God.

The mind of Christ is the goal, but not the means. Christ lived out an example for us to follow and gave us the Holy Spirit to be able to have His mind, the mind of the Spirit. We received this gift when we accepted Jesus as our Savior. But like an unopened gift at Christmas time, many do not walk in the Spirit. We have the mind of Christ. This is a fact. But we will have to learn to walk in the Spirit and deny the flesh.

Through reading *Make Up Your Mind* and doing this study, I pray you have gained an understanding of what you already have, friends. This final week, we will look at how we have the beautiful mind of Christ that Paul wrote about:

"In your relationships with one another, have the same mindset as Christ Jesus: Who, being in very nature God, did not consider equality with God something to be used to his own advantage; rather, he made himself nothing by taking the very nature of a servant, being made in human likeness. And being found in appearance as a man, he humbled himself by becoming obedient to death—even death on a cross" (Philippians 2:5–8 NIV).

Day One: Sweet Repentance

"And Peter said to them, "Repent and be baptized every one of you in the name of Jesus Christ for the forgiveness of your sins, and you will receive the gift of the Holy Spirit."
Acts 2:38 ESV

We cannot put the cart before the horse. Repentance is necessary to access the Spirit-filled life and to experience change. We need the Holy Spirit to do this work and God promises to complete this work in us, too. Repentance is not a one-time event. It is a daily exercise as we examine ourselves in light of God's Word. Our thought life wanders far away from God, but it does so by degrees, sometimes hardly detectable. The plumb line of God's Word convicts us and demonstrates our need for change, leading us to repentance.

Make Up Your Mind (Study Guide)

READ JEREMIAH 17:10.

How does the fact that God sees in your heart and mind motivate your thought life?

_____

_____

I love the fact that Scripture says God rewards us according to our thoughts and deeds! There is no greater motivation than pleasing God!

READ 1 JOHN 1:9.

What role does confession have?

_____

_____

READ PSALM 51:1–4.

What is a key to our repentance?

_____

_____

Sin is deceptive and gives us a hardened heart. But when David was caught in his sin, he displayed true repentance. David was a man after God's own heart who cared that his sin hurt God.

READ PSALM 86:11.

The Psalmist offered many beautiful prayers of repentance. How do we heal our divided hearts?

_____

_____

I once helped a friend walk through betrayal after her husband committed adultery. The pain was immense. But what struck me in the middle of their struggle was true repentance. The husband displayed it so beautifully. Akin to David's response when the prophet Nathan told David that he was the man, the guilty one, my friend's husband bore the marks of true repentance: humility and brokenness. He did not defend himself or make excuses. He did not think he deserved her forgiveness. But she gave it anyway. Their marriage today is one that many look to as a model of grace and passion. Repentance opens the door for healing.

Day Two: Renewing Our Mind

". . . Be renewed in the spirit of your minds."
Ephesians 4:23 ESV

Our culture talks about having a growth mindset as if it was something we could produce on our own. If our hearts are desperately evil (Romans 3:10, Jeremiah 17:9), then how do we have a growth mindset? A growth mindset is not the answer. But the mind of Christ is. Scripture talks about renewing our mind in God's Word and to think like Christ. This is the answer the world so desperately needs. And we play a role in the renewing of our minds, too.

READ EPHESIANS 4:22–24.

How do we get a new attitude in our minds?

_____

_____

We cannot "put on" the new self if we have not first "put off" the old self. What do you need to let go of so you can embrace all God has for you.

READ ROMANS 12:2.

Is transformation something we can accomplish?

_____

_____

We cannot transform ourselves but we will be transformed when we renew our mind by saturating our minds with God's Word.

READ PHILIPPIANS 4:8.

How does thinking on these things help produce mind renewal?

_____

_____

READ 2 CORINTHIANS 4:16.

How often should we renew our mind?

_____

_____

Day Three: Walking in the Spirit

"But I say, walk by the Spirit, and you
will not gratify the desires of the flesh."
Galatians 5:16 ESV

Part of the struggle of walking in the Spirit is due to the familiarity we have of walking in the flesh. It is all we have ever known before we were born again. It is what comes naturally to us. Added to this complication of essentially learning how to walk again is the fact that it is not just unnatural to walk in the Spirit. It is supernatural. And it requires a death. We cannot walk the fence and be both in the Spirit and in the flesh. We need to choose.

READ GALATIANS 5:25.

What must happen in order for us to walk in the Spirit?

_____

_____

Living by the Spirit means we don't follow our feelings like we used to. It means that our walk matches our talk and we live what we say we believe. It means we pray and are

Make Up Your Mind **(Study Guide)**

sensitive to the Spirit's leading. We feed our souls rather than our flesh. But this is made difficult by the war going on within our own mind.

READ GALATIANS 5:17.

How do you determine whether your desires are of the flesh or of the Spirit?

_____

_____

READ ROMANS 8:5.

What our mind is set upon reveals whether we are walking in the Spirit or in the flesh. Sometimes this is seen by our priorities. What is important to you?

_____

_____

READ ROMANS 8:6.

What is the fruit of the mind that is governed by the Spirit?

_____

_____

READ ROMANS 8:9.

What does walking in the Spirit show?

_____

_____

We belong. Those who are in Christ ought to be different from those who are in the world. And it begins in our minds. The world does not need a church that is worldly. It needs a church that is godly, walking in the Spirit, and walking in the mind of Christ. The battle of the mind must be fought in the Spirit and waged with the Word of God.

Day Four: Maintaining Our Minds

"Guard your heart above all else, for it determines the course of your life."
Proverbs 4:23 NLT

When my children were little, I would tell them that bad company corrupts good morals and to abstain from evil. Over time, I noticed a self-righteousness developing in comparing to others. I realized it wasn't right for my children just to stay away from those who did not behave or believe. They should seek to be a light to others and not view themselves as better. We need to protect our belief system and mindset so we don't get sucked into evil, but still there was another component. They were not capable of doing good themselves if their hearts were not first transformed and kept in God's Word. So, we guarded the influences in our home. We guarded the senses—the eye gate and ear gate—and I got my children devotionals until they were coming out of their ears. But maintaining our minds in Christ is never done. We must guard our minds daily so we can help others see.

READ 1 PETER 1:13.

What do we need to set our minds on?

_____

_____

READ 2 TIMOTHY 4:3–4.

What leads people's minds away from God?

_____

_____

The world is deceptive. Our own hearts are deceptive. But listening to truth guards our minds. Being in the Word of God daily helps us to recognize and live by the truth.

READ JOHN 8:31–32.

How does knowing the truth set you free?

_____

_____

Knowing the truth enables us to hold to Christ's teaching and to live it out, no longer enslaved to this world. Tomorrow we will wrap up our study by discovering how identity impacts our ability to be like Jesus.

Day Five: Identity in Christ

*"I have been crucified with Christ. It is no longer
I who live, but Christ who lives in me. And the
life I now live in the flesh I live by faith in the Son
of God, who loved me and gave himself for me."*
Galatians 2:20 ESV

One of the reasons we struggle to walk in the mind of Christ is because we are still conceding to the flesh. That is not our identity anymore. When our identity is in Christ, we live into that identity. We are under new lordship and our mindset is geared toward that identity.

READ 2 CORINTHIANS 5:17.

Do you still tend to identify with the old you?

_____

_____

READ 2 CORINTHIANS 3:18.

Transformation takes time as we continually undergo sanctification. How does this transformation happen?

_____

_____

READ EPHESIANS 4:24–31.

How do you put on the new self?

_____

_____

Putting on our identity in Christ is something we do every day as we seek God and get into His Word. The enemy of our souls does not want us to know our identity. He would like to keep us bound in negative mindsets that cause us to miss the grace of God and waste our lives. But knowing who we are in Christ and whose we are is essential to being able to carry out the mission God has for us.

READ 1 PETER 2:9.

Those who are in Christ are chosen. Christ came to give us His identity, to restore our broken image. What is our purpose as we walk in this identity?

_____

_____

We get to declare Christ to a lost world. What an honor and a privilege. There is no greater purpose. We are sign posts to our Savior! Friend, my prayer is that as we have walked through these mindsets, we have seen that we have a great heritage through the mind of Christ. We must not waste any more time on this earth bound in negative mindsets. Walk in the freedom of Christ and help release others from the bondage of their own minds, too. "Beloved, we are God's children now, and what we will be has not yet appeared; but we know that when he appears we shall be like him, because we shall see him as he is" (1 John 3:2 ESV).

Weekly Wrap-Up

Chapter Twelve Reflection Questions

Which trigger did you identify with the most?

_____

_____

Which tip is your "go to strategy" when it comes to putting on the mind of Christ?

_____

_____

What is the mind of Christ?

_____

_____

The Keys to Mindset Hacks

Write down the keys from chapter twelve and any other insight that was significant to you.

Key Thought

_____

_____

Key Verse

_____

_____

Key Chang

_____

_____

Counselor's Corner

Battling Insecurity and Embracing the Mind of Christ

Mindset Meditation

> *"For, 'Who has known the mind of*
> *the Lord so as to instruct him?'*
> *But we have the mind of Christ."*
> 1 Corinthians 2:16 NIV

As you breathe deeply and find a comfortable position, ask God to show you what it means for you to have the mind of Christ.

Record on the lines below what it means to you to have the "mind of Christ."

_____

_____

_____

_____

Mindset Movement

Describe the transformation you are experiencing as you live daily as that future woman claiming she has the mind of Christ and exchanging her thoughts for God's thoughts.

_____

_____

_____

_____

Questions for Connection:

1. Share what having the "mind of Christ" means to you.
2. What are some aspects of yourself that you could accept grace for and stop being hard on yourself?
3. What's the biggest shift you've seen in your mindset since reading this book?

Additional Resources

Tired of Trying to Measure Up by Jeff VanVonderan
Seeing Yourself Through God's Eyes by June Hunt
Lifetime Guarantee: Making Your Christian Life Work and What to Do When It Doesn't by Bill Gillham

Notes or Questions from Chapter Reading

URL Links to Videos

Study Guide videos: http://makeupyourmind.today/
muym-bible-study-videos
Password: MUYMToday!

Mindset Battle Quiz: https://bit.ly/mindset-battle-quiz
Authors' website: https://makeupyourmind.today/

Appendix A
Scriptures to Help Reset Mindsets

Philippians 2:2-5 ESV

"Complete my joy by being of the same mind, having the same love, being in full accord and of one mind. Do nothing from selfish ambition or conceit, but in humility count others more significant than yourselves. Let each of you look not only to his own interests, but also to the interests of others. Have this mind among yourselves, which is yours in Christ Jesus."

Philippians 4:8 ESV

"Finally, brothers, whatever is true, whatever is honorable, whatever is just, whatever is pure, whatever is lovely, whatever is commendable, if there is any excellence, if there is anything worthy of praise, think about these things."

1 Corinthians 2:16 ESV

"'For who has understood the mind of the Lord so as to instruct Him?' But we have the mind of Christ."

1 Peter 4:1 ESV

"Since therefore Christ suffered in the flesh, arm yourselves with the same way of thinking, for whoever has suffered in the flesh has ceased from sin."

Isaiah 26:3 ESV

"You keep him in perfect peace whose mind is stayed on you, because he trusts in you."

Proverbs 4:23 NLT

"Guard your heart above all else, for it determines the course of your life."

2 Corinthians 10:5 ESV

"We destroy arguments and every lofty opinion raised against the knowledge of God, and take every thought captive to obey Christ."

Romans 12:2 ESV

"Do not be conformed to this world, but be transformed by the renewal of your mind, that by testing you may discern what is the will of God, what is good and acceptable and perfect."

1 Peter 1:13 ESV

"Therefore, preparing your minds for action, and being sober-minded, set your hope fully on the grace that will be brought to you at the revelation of Jesus Christ."

Matthew 22:37 ESV

"And he said to him, 'You shall love the Lord your God with all your heart and with all your soul and with all your mind.'"

Mark 7:20–22 ESV

"And he said, 'What comes out of a person is what defiles him. For from within, out of the heart of man, come evil thoughts, sexual immorality, theft, murder, adultery, coveting, wickedness, deceit, sensuality, envy, slander, pride, foolishness.'"

Galatians 5:16–17 ESV

"But I say, walk by the Spirit, and you will not gratify the desires of the flesh. For the desires of the flesh are against the Spirit, and the desires of the Spirit are against the flesh, for these are opposed to each other, to keep you from doing the things you want to do."

James 1:19–20 ESV

"Know this, my beloved brothers: let every person be quick to hear, slow to speak, slow to anger; for the anger of man does not produce the righteousness of God."

Colossians 3:2 ESV

"Set your minds on things that are above, not on things that are on earth."

Romans 8:5–8 ESV

"For those who live according to the flesh set their minds on the things of the flesh, but those who live according to the Spirit set their minds on the things of the Spirit. For to set the mind on the flesh is death, but to set the mind on the Spirit is life and peace. For the mind that is set on the flesh is hostile to God, for it does not submit to God's law; indeed, it cannot. Those who are in the flesh cannot please God."

James 4:1 ESV

"What causes quarrels and what causes fights among you? Is it not this, that your passions are at war within you?"

Colossians 3:5 ESV

"Put to death therefore what is earthly in you: sexual immorality, impurity, passion, evil desire, and covetousness, which is idolatry."

Acts 3:19 ESV

"Repent therefore, and turn again, that your sins may be blotted out."

Colossians 3:12–14 ESV

"Put on then, as God's chosen ones, holy and beloved, compassionate hearts, kindness, humility, meekness, and patience, bearing with one another and, if one has a complaint against another, forgiving each other; as the Lord has forgiven you, so you also must forgive. And above all these put on love, which binds everything together in perfect harmony."

Ephesians 4:31–32 ESV

"Let all bitterness and wrath and anger and clamor and slander be put away from you, along with all malice. Be kind to one another, tenderhearted, forgiving one another, as God in Christ forgave you."

Proverbs 12:16 ESV

"The vexation of a fool is known at once, but the prudent ignores an insult."

Matthew 15:18–19 ESV

"But what comes out of the mouth proceeds from the heart, and this defiles a person. For out of the heart come evil thoughts, murder, adultery, sexual immorality, theft, false witness, slander."

Galatians 6:7–8 ESV

"Do not be deceived: God is not mocked, for whatever one sows, that will he also reap. For the one who sows to his own flesh will from the flesh reap corruption, but the one who sows to the Spirit will from the Spirit reap eternal life."

Proverbs 15:1 ESV

"A soft answer turns away wrath, but a harsh word stirs up anger."

Romans 15:1–2 ESV

"We who are strong have an obligation to bear with the failings of the weak, and not to please ourselves. Let each of us please his neighbor for his good, to build him up."

Proverbs 15:7 ESV

"The lips of the wise spread knowledge; not so the hearts of fools."

James 1:22 ESV

"But be doers of the word, and not hearers only, deceiving yourselves."

Romans 12:1 ESV

"I appeal to you therefore, brothers, by the mercies of God, to present your bodies as a living sacrifice, holy and acceptable to God, which is your spiritual worship."

Ephesians 4:26 ESV

"Be angry and do not sin; do not let the sun go down on your anger."

1 Corinthians 2:14 ESV

"The natural person does not accept the things of the Spirit of God, for they are folly to him, and he is not able to understand them because they are spiritually discerned."

Matthew 5:28 ESV

"But I say to you that everyone who looks at a woman with lustful intent has already committed adultery with her in his heart."

Proverbs 11:3 ESV

The integrity of the upright guides them, but the crookedness of the treacherous destroys them.

Ephesians 2:1–3 ESV

"And you were dead in the trespasses and sins in which you once walked, following the course of this world, following the prince of the power of the air, the spirit that is now at work in the sons of disobedience—among whom we all once lived in the passions of our flesh, carrying out the desires of the body."

Appendix B
Living Out the Mindset of Christ

Living into the reality of the mind of Christ will take practice because we have been trained to adapt to the mentality of the culture around us. Shame and fear of man keep us bound in mindsets and impact our lives in profound ways unless we know how to break free.

Our mindset affects how we live in relationship with others. When we are not easily offended and seek to help one another have Christ's perspective, we honor God in our relationships. Paul exhorts us to have the mind of Christ as concerns our relationships: "In your relationships with one another, have the same mindset as Christ Jesus" (Philippians 2:5 NIV). Christ came to serve others in humility. When we become offended, we serve self and are blindsided by pride. But when we love the people in our life, we seek to steward that relationship by not allowing negative mindsets to interfere with the sweet fellowship we can have in Christ.

To help with adopting the mind of Christ, the resources provided here in the appendix will guide you in unlocking mindsets, praying with the mindset of Christ, recognizing worldviews that pull us away from the mind of Christ, and Scriptures to help us fight what is really a spiritual battle.

"When we tell you these things, we do not use words that come from human wisdom. Instead, we speak words given to us by the Spirit, using the Spirit's words to explain spiritual truths. But people who aren't spiritual can't receive these truths from God's Spirit. It all sounds foolish to them and they can't understand it,

Make Up Your Mind (Study Guide)

for only those who are spiritual can understand what the Spirit means. Those who are spiritual can evaluate all things, but they themselves cannot be evaluated by others. For, 'Who can know the Lord's thoughts? Who knows enough to teach him?' But we understand these things, for we have the mind of Christ" (1 Corinthians 2:13–16 NLT).

Appendix C
Unlocking Mindsets

Hopefully by now we are learning that negative mindsets are a prison within our own minds, and we hold the key to be set free from them. When we encounter a negative mindset, we have a choice whether we will adopt it. However, sometimes we don't recognize our choice in the matter. When we are beset by a mindset, perhaps in a panicky situation, we are not thinking straight enough to overcome that mindset. Below is a step-by-step method to help free us from a negative mindset so we can walk in the Spirit and not the flesh.

Step No. 1: Determine the mindset.

Ask yourself questions to figure out what mindset is at play.

- What precipitated or led to the mindset?
- What was your response to that trigger?
- What core emotion are you feeling? Anger? Sadness? Confusion?
- Who is the dominant player in your mind? You or someone else?

Step No. 2: Listen to the self-talk in your brain.

Just because you think a thought does not make it true.

- Does it sound like a particular mindset or the mind of Christ?
- Jot down the lies and replace them with truth.

Make Up Your Mind (Study Guide)

Step No. 3: Was the mindset provoked by an offense?

Hurt feelings can get our adrenaline going and cause us to lose perspective.

- What about the trigger was offensive?
- Is the offense brought on by presumption or something more concrete?

Step No. 4: Change the focus.

Self can cause us to become myopic. Try to think outside of yourself.

- Mindsets become entrenched when you give them fuel by rehearsing the matter over and over in your mind.
- Serve somebody else and take the focus off yourself.

Step No. 5: Be grateful.

Focusing on the negative can be overwhelming. Find something to be grateful for.

- Start with what you normally take for granted.
- Worship, praise, and thank God even amid the pain. Worship brings clarity.

Step No. 6: Put on Christ.

We must put off before we put on. Below are things to help renew your mind.

- Think on how Christ would handle the situation.
- Let God be your defender.
- Pray about the situation. Participate in spiritual warfare prayer, in accordance with God's will.

- Pick one or two verses that speak to the situation and meditate on them.
- Decide how you are going to respond. Choose to deny the flesh and walk in the Spirit.

Helping Others

We must put our own proverbial oxygen masks on to be able to help others breathe. Sometimes when someone else is experiencing a negative mindset, we can be drawn in by it, or we can try to help them snap out of it. Mindsets are often unreasonable and overly dramatic, as well as stubborn. They are spiritual strongholds. Breaking someone else free from them requires discernment and patience. Helping someone who is in a negative mindset recognize and see a way out is difficult but not impossible. When we think according to the flesh, we cannot understand or discern the spiritual battle all around us. Below are some steps to help someone gain discernment and overcome a negative mindset before it inflicts further damage.

Step No. 1: Listen.

Listen to them. Don't be quick to provide an answer. They cannot hear and are close-minded until they know they have been heard. We need to help them understand that just because they might feel justified to remain in a certain thought pattern, they are the ones held prisoner by that mindset. For instance, when we are mistreated or disrespected, the boastful pride of life rises within us, and we can become angry or insecure.

Step No. 2: Agree.

Agree that their feelings are undeniably understandable but encourage them to lay down their "right" to their feelings, just like Jesus did. Have compassion for them and tell them about the positive ways they are handling the problem as affirming stepping stones.

Step No. 3: Expose.

Expose the lies of the mindset. Try to help them see wrong thinking and where their hurt might be preventing them from seeing things clearly.

Step No. 4: Find biblical truth.

Look for truth in the situation. Take self out of the equation. Recognize it is a spiritual matter. Our battle is not against the flesh. Find applicable Scriptures to share with them. Encourage them to lay down their own thoughts and pick up God's.

Step No. 5: Show the mind of Christ.

Find how Christ dealt with the same mindset. Pray with them to be victorious over the mindset and to have the mind of Christ.

Appendix D
Praying with the Mindset of Christ

Christ taught us how to pray. Yet we can say the words by heart without really understanding the significance of His prayer. Praying with the mindset of Christ means praying in humility and laying down our will. Below is the prayer that Jesus gave as an example to pray. It can help center us in His will rather than in the mindset wars that so easily beset us. There are seven petitions in this prayer. Let's pray them together in a fresh new way as we release the negative mindsets of this world and adopt Christ's instead.

Pray, then, in this way: Our Father who is in heaven, Hallowed be Your name. Your kingdom come. Your will be done, on earth as it is in heaven. Give us this day our daily bread. And forgive us our debts, as we also have forgiven our debtors. And do not lead us into temptation, but deliver us from evil (Matthew 6:9–13 NASB).

1. Hallowed be your name

"There is none holy like the LORD; for there is none besides you; there is no rock like our God." 1 Samuel 2:2 ESV

Thinking on lesser things keeps us bound in the flesh. Reflecting on the perfection and greatness of our God frees us from the dominion of the lesser things. God is perfect. His ways are perfect. When we honor God as holy in our lives, our lives are in order. In this prayer, we acknowledge God's righteousness and His position in our lives.

Make Up Your Mind (Study Guide)

2. **Your kingdom come**

"But seek first the kingdom of God and his righteousness, and all these things will be added to you." Matthew 6:33 ESV

This world is not our hope. When we get caught up in trying to make a fallen world like Heaven, we will be disappointed. Desiring God's will and His kingdom to come reminds us we are not living for the here and now. God has set eternity in the heart of man. Fixing our minds on His kingdom purposes frees us from the world's pull on us.

3. **Your will be done on earth as it is in Heaven**

"Do not be conformed to this world, but be transformed by the renewal of your mind, that by testing you may discern what is the will of God, what is good and acceptable and perfect." Romans 12:2 ESV

Negative mindsets cause us to be focused on our will. Praying this petition is an opportunity to seek to live for Christ, not self. Surrendering to God's purposes, even when they don't align with ours, sets us free to live for God's will.

4. **Give us this day our daily bread**

"I have not departed from the commandment of his lips; I have treasured the words of his mouth more than my portion of food." Job 23:12 ESV

What we think about impacts our desires. As we come before God, do we want more than His portion for us? Or are we content with His provision? Thanking God for what He provides and emptying ourselves of our wants helps us to have a grateful mindset.

5. **Forgive us our debts, as we also have forgiven our debtors**

> *"For if you forgive others their trespasses, your heavenly Father will also forgive you, but if you do not forgive others their trespasses, neither will your Father forgive your trespasses."* Matthew 6:14-15 ESV

A bitter, unforgiving mindset will hinder our prayers. We can release the offense against others because we recognize we are just as guilty. Unforgiveness hurts us. And it hurts the heart of God who died for every sin. Can we not forgive what He already has? Peace is the result when we let go of hurts in Jesus' name.

6. Lead us not into temptation

> *"Let no one say when he is tempted, 'I am being tempted by God,' for God cannot be tempted with evil, and he himself tempts no one. But each person is tempted when he is lured and enticed by his own desire. Then desire when it has conceived gives birth to sin, and sin when it is fully grown brings forth death."* James 1:13–15 ESV

As we ask God to help us overcome temptation, we need to choose carefully what we think on. Our desires give birth to sin. God can only lead those who will be led. Replacing sinful, negative thoughts with thinking on what is true, noble, right, pure, lovely, admirable, excellent, or praiseworthy (Philippians 4:8) helps us overcome the temptation to be fixated on the negative and therefore to overcome the resulting sin from those thoughts.

7. Deliver us from evil

"They do not fear bad news; they confidently trust the LORD to care for them." Psalm 112:7 NLT

As we ask God to protect us from evil, we also need to recognize the evil resident within our own minds. Our minds are powerful and able to pull us away from God. The mindset of fear holds many captive. As we trust God to take care of us, we have joy. "I sought the LORD, and he answered me and delivered me from all my fears" (Psalm 34:4 ESV).

Appendix E
Examining Worldviews

A worldview is simply the lens through which we view the world. It is defined by our belief system, which frames the decisions we make. Our worldview affects all of life. A worldview is not just our perspective; it is how that perspective shapes our lives. We have seen how our experiences, environment, and thought life form our mindset. We don't question it because it is our normal. It's our "truth," part of our belief system. When someone challenges that mindset, it is as if we are not capable of thinking outside of that norm.

Adding to our own mindset battles are the worldviews surrounding us, seeking to lull us away from a biblical foundation. We have battles within and battles without. What is a mind to do? First and foremost, we are to get informed and renewed by the Word of God. When we let the Bible shape our mindset and value system, we can recognize a counterfeit worldview.

Rewiring Our Brains

Thought patterns form paths in our brain. We need to form new paths. We do that as we reset our mindset through the Word of God. Part of healing our mindsets is addressing the worldviews we have ascribed to as well. In essence, we need to calibrate our worldview to a biblical one. We need to recognize where we have shifted from God's way. The culture surrounding us does not have the Bible as its authority. It has self on the throne. Ultimately, worldviews form strongholds in the mindsets of people. A stronghold is a lie that keeps us trapped because we believe in it. However, we get to choose what we believe. To do so, we must recognize the lies and debunk the strongholds in our mind.

Determining the Strongholds

To find the strongholds we need to get with God and ask the why questions. Why are we anxious? Why are we angry? Why are we sad? When we keep asking why, we will drill down to the stronghold. Then we can worship God right in the middle of that stronghold in our mind. A by-product of giving praise to God is our mind being set free from strongholds. Friends, we must make up our mind to live out and protect our belief system. The enemy of our soul attacks the mind so he can create doubt and confusion. As we demolish strongholds, we discover the foundation of that stronghold: the worldview it is attached to.

Demolishing Strongholds and Pretensions

"We use God's mighty weapons, not worldly weapons, to knock down the strongholds of human reasoning and to destroy false arguments." 2 Corinthians 10:4 NLT

We are not powerless unless we don't stay in the battle. God has given us what we need to fight the spiritual warfare in our mind and in our culture. It will be a fight. Thought patterns can become entrenched, but God can renew our minds. We just have to know how to break strongholds. We can demolish arguments with truth. We must be in God's Word to be able to transform our minds. As we study Scripture, we can worship God and declare His truths. This will reframe our mind and demolish the lies.

Identify the Stronghold

> *"For the weapons of our warfare are not of the flesh but have divine power to destroy strongholds."* 2 Corinthians 10:4 ESV

We must ask questions and search Scripture. We can ask loved ones to help us define what our chief worldview is. God will help us defeat the stronghold in our life.

Take Captive Every Thought

> *"We demolish arguments and every pretension that sets itself up against the knowledge of God, and we take captive every thought to make it obedient to Christ."* 2 Corinthians 10:5 NIV

We can cast all our anxiety on Christ for He cares for us. As we put our thoughts through the truth filter of the Bible, we can ask ourselves if our thoughts and values line up with God's Word.

Understanding Worldviews

As we grapple with the strongholds in our minds, we need to address the belief system behind it all. Worldviews are a matter of the heart and how we see the world. They frame how we process our thoughts and values. We need to recognize not just the mindset struggle we are having, but also the worldview system behind that mindset. Be aware of other worldviews so you are not ensnared by them.

ENDNOTES

[1] http://www.mountvernon.org/library/quotes/article/it-is-better-to-offer-no-excuse-than-a-bad-one/

Make Up Your Mind (Study Guide)

Make Up Your Mind (Study Guide)